# GRACE MOMENTS
## APRIL–JUNE 2025

Published by Straight Talk Books
P.O. Box 301, Milwaukee, WI 53201
800.661.3311 / timeofgrace.org

Copyright © 2025 Time of Grace Ministry

All rights reserved. This publication may not be copied, photocopied, reproduced, translated, or converted to any electronic or machine-readable form in whole or in part, except for brief quotations, without prior written approval from Time of Grace Ministry.

Unless otherwise indicated, Scripture is taken from THE HOLY BIBLE, NEW INTERNATIONAL VERSION®. NIV®. Copyright © 1973, 1978, 1984, 2011 by Biblica, Inc.® Used by permission. All rights reserved worldwide.

Scripture marked CSB is taken from the Christian Standard Bible. Copyright © 2017 by Holman Bible Publishers. Used by permission. Christian Standard Bible®, and CSB® are federally registered trademarks of Holman Bible Publishers, all rights reserved.

Scripture marked EHV is taken from the Holy Bible, Evangelical Heritage Version® (EHV®) © 2019 Wartburg Project, Inc. All rights reserved. Used by permission.

Scripture marked ESV is taken from the ESV® Bible (The Holy Bible, English Standard Version®). ESV® Text Edition: 2016. Copyright © 2001 by Crossway, a publishing ministry of Good News Publishers. The ESV® text has been reproduced in cooperation with and by permission of Good News Publishers. Unauthorized reproduction of this publication is prohibited. All rights reserved.

Scripture marked KJV is taken from the King James Version. Text is public domain.

Scripture marked MSG is taken from *THE MESSAGE*, copyright © 1993, 2002, 2018 by Eugene H. Peterson. Used by permission of NavPress. All rights reserved. Represented by Tyndale House Publishers, Inc.

Scripture marked NLT is taken from the *Holy Bible*, New Living Translation, copyright © 1996, 2004, 2015 by Tyndale House Foundation. Used by permission of Tyndale House Publishers, Inc., Carol Stream, Illinois 60188. All rights reserved.

Scripture marked TLB is taken from The Living Bible, copyright © 1971 by Tyndale House Foundation. Used by permission of Tyndale House Publishers Inc., Carol Stream, Illinois 60188. All rights reserved. The Living Bible, TLB, and The Living Bible logo are registered trademarks of Tyndale House Publishers.

Printed in the United States of America
ISBN: 978-1-965694-16-9

TIME OF GRACE *is a registered mark of Time of Grace Ministry.*

# APRIL

For since we believe that Jesus died and rose again, even so, through Jesus, God will bring with him those who have fallen asleep.

1 THESSALONIANS 4:14

April 1

## Why would God let you in?
Mike Novotny

A few weeks ago, my friend had a dream in which he died, was whisked to heaven, and stood before God himself. That's when God asked him, "Why should I let you in?" At that very moment, my friend woke up.

"Pastor, I've been thinking about that question ever since it happened," he confessed.

That's the right question. Is heaven really for people like us? God knows all things, which means he knows everything wrong we have ever done (we tend to forget 99.999% of our sins, don't we?). And God hates all sins, which means he feels about every sin the way we feel about the most grotesque sins (child abuse, extortion, violence, racism). If those two things are true, why would God let you and me in?

Here's a one-word answer: *Jesus.* On the first Easter, Jesus appeared to Mary Magdalene, a woman with some seriously heavy moral baggage, and told her, **"Do not be afraid"** (Matthew 28:10). Then he told her to pass a message on to **"my brothers,"** a shocking phrase given that Peter and company had just abandoned/denied Jesus in his greatest time of need.

These words teach us how to get into heaven: Not by being good people. Not by learning from our mistakes. Not by avoiding the "big sins." The way to get into heaven is Jesus. Repent of your sins, believe in his name, and you will know what to say when your last breath comes.

Why would God let you into heaven? The only answer that works is Jesus.

**April 2**

# Who is the Easter bunny?
## Daron Lindemann

Who is the Easter bunny anyway? And how did a rabbit become connected to the resurrection of Jesus Christ?

In A.D. 595, monks from Rome were sent to England to convert the Anglo-Saxons to Christianity. The monks convinced the pagan Britons to integrate their ancient celebrations with Christian festivities. Their worship of Eostre, the goddess of springtime, was already associated with rabbits, pastels, and springtime celebrations. So Easter and rabbits came together as a mission effort.

The legend of the Easter bunny came to the U.S. through the traditions of German immigrants who settled there in the 1700s. Over time, the Easter bunny and the hunt for his Easter eggs have become an Easter tradition, especially for children. By the way, in other ancient cultures, rabbits were associated with rebirth and new life because of their prolific fertility. Sometimes people would include rabbits on their gravestones.

Although there is no direct biblical connection between Jesus and rabbits, his resurrection promises new life! **"If anyone is in Christ, the new creation has come: The old has gone, the new is here!"** (2 Corinthians 5:17). And these furry, multiplying creatures inspire Christians to multiply too, as we **"make disciples"** (Matthew 28:19).

Is the Easter bunny a secular attempt to distract from the true meaning of Easter? The answer is up to you. You can thoughtfully leverage the history, tradition, and symbolism of our rabbit friend—especially to teach children. Or you can celebrate Easter without something furry.

April 3

# Witnesses of God's goodness
## Andrea Delwiche

What does it mean to give witness to the greatness of God? Here's one biblical example: **"Praise the name of God, praise the works of God. I, too, give witness to the greatness of God, our Lord, high above all other gods"** (Psalm 135:1,5 MSG).

God spreads a table of bounty from which we taste and see his perfection at work in the world around us. The bright or tender smiles of our loved ones, the smooth agility of a gifted athlete, a gallery of well-executed oil paintings, or a child's bright and simple finger painting each testify to God's goodness. The water and Word in Baptism and the presence of Christ in the bread and wine of Lord's Supper testify to God's provision.

Christ's self-giving life and death and his stunning defeat of death are the flowering that frees us. We can be like a bright-eyed and curious child who's safe on a parent's lap, safe to notice and speak about all we see. Additionally, we have at least some agency in choosing what in life gets our time and attention.

Jesus speaks of this succinctly in the gospel of Matthew: **"For the mouth speaks what the heart is full of. A good man brings good things out of the good stored up in him, and an evil man brings evil things out of the evil stored up in him"** (Matthew 12:34,35). We will be witnesses of God's goodness if we fill our days and our hearts with noticing, remembering, and praising the works of God.

**April 4**

## It's a war zone
### Mike Novotny

Do you ever think about spiritual warfare? About the war zone your soul woke up to and walked into this morning? About the cosmic battle between God and the devil over the state of your faith? Maybe. Or maybe you thought today was just . . . life. A randomly good (or not so good) spiritual day.

According to the Bible, because you have a soul that God loves and the devil wants, today is much more than that. It is a war zone of obedience or indulgence, of holiness or rebellion, of exalting God or minimizing his glory. This battlefield is where you pick up your Bible or you don't, where you remember to pray or forget, where you share your faith or keep the good news to yourself, where you serve your neighbor or just keep serving yourself. All of that, every spiritual victory or defeat, is a result of the very real war zone that you live in.

The apostle Paul opens our eyes to the reality of this war when he writes, **"For our struggle is not against flesh and blood, but against the rulers, against the authorities, against the powers of this dark world and against the spiritual forces of evil in the heavenly realms"** (Ephesians 6:12).

It's hard to win a war when you don't realize you are in one. Pray today that God would open your eyes to the evil around you and that through the impenetrable armor of Jesus' love he would help you fight this good fight and stand firm in your faith!

**April 5**

# You'll be found
C.L. Whiteside

In a world and culture where the desire to advance, receive promotions, and get recognition is high, people say, "You need to find a way to get a seat at the table!" But this doesn't mean stepping on others or resorting to whatever it takes to secure that seat.

Whether you're content or want more, it's important to be faithful with the small things and embrace whatever role you have right now. When an opportunity is in alignment with God's plan for you to be somewhere or hold a certain position, often the only thing that slows the process down or messes it up is you stepping outside of God's will.

In 1 Samuel 16, a young man named David didn't have a seat at the table and wasn't even present when the prophet Samuel came to anoint a new king. Samuel had to send for David. David was tending to sheep. Some might consider that lowly work. It's not the ideal path for being a king or one of the most influential figures of his time.

Our Shepherd, Jesus, loves us more than we can fathom and will find us wherever we are. This is why we can trust in his timing and follow his path faithfully. There's no need to rush the process or deviate from God's will. Matthew 25:21 serves as a reminder: **"His master replied, 'Well done, good and faithful servant! You have been faithful with a few things; I will put you in charge of many things. Come and share your master's happiness!'"**

**April 6**

## Anchored to the rock
Ann Jahns

If you've ever been swimming in the ocean, you know you need to approach it with equal parts respect and awe and a healthy dash of fear. After all, there are creatures in the ocean that can kill you. In addition, the very foundation under your feet can betray you. In seconds, the sandbar you are standing on can be swept away in a crashing wave, leaving you blindly tossed in a riptide and not sure which way is up.

Does your life sometimes feel this way? Do your changing circumstances and shifting emotions ever leave you reeling?

When the ground under your feet keeps moving, it's hard to know what to cling to. And the longer you live on this earth, the more you realize that nothing in it—not friends or spouse or children or money or institutions—can provide the stable foundation you need. Friends can hurt you, spouses can betray you, and children can wander away from you. Your finances can run out. Institutions can fail.

If that's the case, what can you cling to? The book of Hebrews says, **"We have this hope as an anchor for the soul, firm and secure"** (6:19). What is that hope? It is Jesus: our lifeline, our buoy, our unmovable rock. Our unshakable, grounded anchor. Our Savior, who died to join us to our heavenly Father forever.

When the sand shifts beneath your feet and you feel like you are drowning, anchor yourself to Christ. He promises to hold you fast always.

## April 7

# Pour generously
### Jan Gompper

I'm a strict recipe follower. I can't cook anything without measuring out every ingredient to a T. I'm afraid that if I don't, my dish will be a flop. As a result, I don't really like cooking because it's a rather painstaking experience.

My husband, on the other hand, is comfortable grabbing ingredients and making a new tasty treat from scratch, not knowing what the outcome will be. This freedom makes his cooking experience a joyful one.

Some people (even Christ followers) measure out their love as carefully as I measure out ingredients. Depending on the recipient, the portion of love they dole out may vary.

Theologian and philosopher St. Augustine wrote, "The measure of love is to love without measure." He clearly understood that he was a recipient of the measureless, undeserved love of God. And because God freely poured out the fullness of his love by sending his Son to die for the sins of the whole world, we in turn are to dole out our love for one another without measure.

The apostle Paul put it like this: **"May you have the power to understand, as all God's people should, how wide, how long, how high, and how deep his love is. May you experience the love of Christ, though it is too great to understand fully. Then you will be made complete with all the fullness of life and power that comes from God"** (Ephesians 3:18,19 NLT).

The ingredient our world needs most is the love of Christ.

Pour generously!

April 8

## Worth our best
Nathan Nass

How much is God worth to you? Have you ever heard how much God was worth to King David in the Bible? David made plans for a temple to be built for God in Jerusalem. He gave the first gifts toward the building of the temple and encouraged his leaders to do the same. The Bible tells us that David gave 3,000 talents of gold for the temple (1 Chronicles 29:4). That would be equal to about 110 tons or 220,000 pounds of gold. That was David's freewill offering to God, plus lots of silver too.

Do you know how much 220,000 pounds of gold would be worth today? The price of gold is always changing, but it's usually worth at least $2,000 per *ounce*. So 220,000 pounds of gold would be worth about $10,000,000,000 in today's money. That's 10 billion dollars!

Is God worth that much? David's resounding answer was Yes! Actually, David's love for God shone even more brightly in the prayer he prayed as he gave his gift: **"But who am I, and who are my people, that we should be able to give as generously as this? Everything comes from you, and we have given you only what comes from your hand"** (1 Chronicles 29:14).

What an attitude! Everything we have comes from God. Our money, our homes, our cars, our eternal salvation through faith in Jesus. They're all gifts from God. God is worth our best and greatest gifts to him.

April 9

## Spend time *in* the tomb
Linda Buxa

In our modern culture, family members might be buried *near* each other but not *with* each other. But if you were an ancient Israelite, it was important to be buried *with* your ancestors. When Jacob was dying, he said, **"Bury me with my fathers"** (Genesis 49:29), and his son Joseph honored his request. A man named Barzillai explained he was old and probably no longer helpful in service to David, so he asked to go back home, **"that I may die in my own town [and be buried] near the tomb of my father and mother"** (2 Samuel 19:37). So many people were buried in family tombs that caves had shelves inside.

Knowing that tradition helps me understand Romans 6:3-5 better: **"Or don't you know that all of us who were baptized into Christ Jesus were baptized into his death? We were therefore *buried with him* through baptism into death in order that, just as Christ was raised from the dead through the glory of the Father, we too may live a new life. For if we have been united with him in a death like his, we will certainly also be united with him in a resurrection like his."**

What a picture! When you were baptized in the name of the Father, Son, and Holy Spirit, your sins were washed away because you have been buried with Jesus. Then because he was raised to life, he gives you that new life too. Because you've already been in the tomb with him, you get to live forever in glory with him too.

April 10

## Big things and Jesus
### Daron Lindemann

Why do you pay $185 for a concert ticket when you can watch and listen to songs on YouTube? Why take a Disney cruise when the kids can binge the Disney Channel at home? One word: *Bigness*. And where you have bigness, you have more. More discoveries and delights. More options and opportunities.

Why do you need worship at church when you can sing praises to Jesus at home? One word: *Bigness*. In worship at church, you worship Jesus more. You wear a cross on your necklace, but that's nothing compared to the big cross at church! If you are physically able yet not in worship at church, you are worshiping Jesus less. If you are in worship at church, you are worshiping Jesus more.

Before Jesus was born, King Herod renovated and massively expanded the Jewish temple. He increased the size of the temple mount platform to 40 acres (25 football fields). He employed 10,000 men, and it took approximately 10 years to build. The small-size limestone building blocks he quarried weighed 2 to 5 tons; the big ones were 10 times that. The temple contained what might be the largest one-piece quarried stone in history: 41 feet long, 11 feet high, and weighing 370 tons.

That's bigness! But it's nothing compared to Jesus.

How big is Jesus to you? How big are his promises? His mission? Jesus, referring to himself as Savior, says it all: **"I tell you that something greater than the temple is here"** (Matthew 12:6). Worship big!

April 11

## Already?
Jason Nelson

"The days of our years are threescore years and ten; and if by reason of strength they be fourscore years . . . it is soon cut off, and we fly away" (Psalm 90:10 KJV).

When I read this passage as a child, it seemed like a hypothetical proposition. The age of 70 or 80 is the age of grandpas and dirt. Hard to relate to as a child. Certainly nothing to be concerned about. But this summer my wife, Nancy, and I will turn 70. If my math is right, that is three score and ten. And the shelf life of my new heart valve is about ten years, give or take. So for me, this is all starting to add up. I was putting off getting new church jeans until the ones I have are more faded. But I think I'll go shopping.

Many of us are in this late decade of constant carefulness. We know we need to be prepared but are just not sure what to be prepared for. One false step, and it could be over. So Nancy and I are cross-training each other just in case.

It's also the decade of reflection and gratitude. **"I have been young, and now am old; yet have I not seen the righteous forsaken, nor his seed begging bread"** (Psalm 37:25 KJV). We've lived long enough to tell the stories of God's faithfulness to us.

I know someday God's gonna come knockin' on my door and say, "Jason, it's time to fly." And I suspect I'll say, "Already?"

April 12

## How to stand up to Satan
Mike Novotny

God's goal for you today is to stand up to the devil. That's why he inspired Paul to write, **"Therefore put on the full armor of God, so that when the day of evil comes, you may be able to stand your ground, and after you have done everything, to stand"** (Ephesians 6:13). Study Ephesians 6:10-14, and you'll find the word *stand* four separate times, including twice in this single verse.

But how do you do that? If the devil knows your weaknesses and doesn't announce "the day" he will launch his assault on your faith, how do you stand up for Jesus? Paul gives you a hint: "After you have done everything, to stand."

In studying the context, I found four keys for this spiritual war: You stand up to Satan by (1) passages, (2) prayers, (3) people, and (4) a Person. Passages from the Word of Truth protect you from the devil's lies. Prayers are heard and answered by the God who gives you strength. People are fellow soldiers who watch your back and fight by your side. The Person is Jesus, who crushed the devil's head and won the war to save your soul.

Think of a spiritual struggle you are currently dealing with (pride, worry, bitterness, busyness, etc.). What would it look like for you to do all four of those key things? What would change in your weekly habits? Think deeply about these questions because after you have done everything, you will be able to stand.

**April 13**

# Ready or not
Jon Enter

Do you sometimes wish Jesus would just return already? It's bad out there! And it seems to be trending toward worse.

Jesus taught that he will come back to earth **"in clouds with great power and glory"** (Mark 13:26). That's so different from Jesus' first coming at Christmas when only a few shepherds knew he had arrived. When Jesus returns on judgment day, he'll be in clouds for all to see his almighty power, and evil will be wiped forever from the earth.

Many first-century Christians were convinced Jesus would return in their lifetime. My grandpa thought the same. Jesus might come back next Thursday. Or it might be another two thousand or more years.

In Mark 13:33, Jesus re-centers the hearts of his listeners then and now by saying, **"Be on guard! Be alert! You do not know when that time will come."** You are alert and ready if you trust that Jesus is your Savior from sin and your only path to paradise in heaven. If Jesus is the center of your heart, that changes how you see the world around you. Evil will come, but it will be undone by Jesus.

It's okay to wish for Jesus to return and show his power. That's your faith wanting God's glory and God's will to be done. And his will ultimately and always will be done. His will is to usher you and all who believe to join him in glory. Come, Lord Jesus!

**April 14**

# Turn away from your cr@p idols
Linda Buxa

I don't envy the prophet Ezekiel who lived at a time when the Israelites were not following God's will. At one point, some leaders wanted to hear from God, so they visited Ezekiel—and he had to pass along a hard message.

"**Then the word of the L**ORD **came to me. 'Son of man, these men have set up their filthy idols in their hearts, and they have placed a stumbling block that makes them guilty in front of their faces. So should I really let them consult me?'**" God mentions their filthy idols four more times and says, "**Repent and turn away from your filthy idols, and turn your faces away from all your abominations**" (Ezekiel 14:2-6 EHV).

God doesn't sugarcoat his message, but English translations do. When God says "filthy idols," he's using the word *gillulim*, which means *idols made from round things*. Those "round things" are dung balls. So God is calling their idols a four-letter word for excrement.

God is clear that anything in our hearts that gets placed above him is a filthy idol. Maybe it's your drinking, workaholic tendencies, constant worry, or love of sports or a political party above everything. The problem is that we easily justify our behavior, which means we all need an Ezekiel in our lives. We need someone brave enough to be honest that God—the jealous God who formed us—says we need to get rid of our cr@p idols.

P.S. We are also called to love others enough that we are an Ezekiel to them too.

**April 15**

## A word nerd's good news
Nate Wordell

As a shameless word nerd, I must tell you about my favorite bit of grammar: the PERFECT PASSIVE PARTICIPLE. If verb terms don't ignite fireworks in your brain, let me tell you why this one can.

A *participle* is an adjective that describes action, like *running* or *smiling*. God has described you with some action-packed participles.

The most precious participles are *passive*, not active. Passive ones describe what someone else did to you. That's good news because you can't mess it up. If you are *hugged*, someone else is doing the work. God is working for you.

Here's the best thing about perfect passive participles: They are *perfect*. In grammar terms, *perfect* means something is a done deal. It's so perfectly completed in the past that it affects you to this day. In the present tense, you are being loved. In the past tense, you once were loved. But in the perfect tense, you were loved in a way that changed everything forever afterward. So, I have to share the perfect passive participles God used to describe you.

In Matthew 25:34, King Jesus says, **"Come, you who are blessed by my Father."** That adjective describes an action God did for you!

Colossians 2:7 says you are **"*rooted* and *built up* in [Christ], strengthened in the faith as you were taught."** You get to be passive because God planted your roots in Jesus.

Ephesians 2:8 promises **"it is by grace you have been saved."** And that's a participle so perfect that it affects you even today.

**April 16**

# A lasting memory
## Clark Schultz

When you gather with family for a meal, do you ever reminisce? Maybe you sift through the memories of meals past. The time when the turkey got burned or the time when someone dropped the stuffing on the floor.

When Jesus gathered in the upper room with his disciples the week before he died, it was to commemorate the Passover—to remember when the Jews were slaves in Egypt and when God liberated them with one last plague (see Exodus 12-13). He went throughout Egypt to kill all the firstborn sons of the Egyptians, but he "passed over" the homes of the Israelites because they had lamb's blood painted on their doorposts.

At Jesus' last Passover meal, he gave his disciples a new memory when he instituted the Lord's Supper: **"Do this in remembrance of me"** (Luke 22:19). Jesus did not just want his disciples to look backward. He gave them and us a lasting memory of his sacrifice on a cross in this sacrament. Why? Because we all have memories we wish we could forget, sins that plague our minds and trouble our hearts.

Jesus has given us the assurance through his body and blood that is in, with, and under the bread and wine that all those sins *are forgiven.* God's anger passes over us. The past does not define us, but our status by the blood of the Lamb shed for us on Calvary does. Rejoice that Christ has given us a memory that lasts.

**April 17**

# The ultimate meal
Clark Schultz

What is your favorite meal? I'm a dessert-first guy—pecan pie or scotcheroos—then meat, potatoes, or—if dieting—a good healthy salad. Jesus gathered with his disciples for one last Passover meal before completing his mission on earth. They ate what the Israelites ate on the very first Passover: **"Meat roasted over the fire, along with bitter herbs, and bread made without yeast"** (Exodus 12:8). They also drank wine.

But then Jesus instituted a new Supper, one where Jesus gives us food that lasts—along with the bread and wine is his body stricken and afflicted for us and his blood shed so God's anger over sin would "pass over" us.

This is the ultimate meal! Why? The apostle Paul tells us: **"Is not the cup of thanksgiving for which we give thanks a participation in the blood of Christ? And is not the bread that we break a participation in the body of Christ?"** (1 Corinthians 10:16). When we join in the Lords Supper, we receive the true body and blood of our Savior Jesus in, with, and under the bread and wine. It's 100% Jesus' body and blood and 100% bread and wine, a remembrance of his sacrifice once and for all for our sins.

Through the Lord's Supper, we get the ultimate meal—our sins forgiven and our faith strengthened. You might have your favorite meal, but only the Supper our Lord gives truly satisfies.

**April 18**

## Who's coming for dinner?
Clark Schultz

A good meal involves the people who join you in that meal—friends, children home for the holidays, or even distant family. At the original Passover, households were to gather fully dressed and ready to go because the Israelites' exodus from Egypt was coming swiftly.

In the upper room before he died, Jesus celebrated Passover with his closest friends. The book of Acts describes these men as **"unschooled, ordinary men"** (4:13). These men were not perfect. In fact, after the supper, this group would run in the opposite direction of Jesus, deny him, and even betray him. In his omniscience, Jesus still ate, drank, and enjoyed their company.

Maybe it is you or someone close to you who has run in the opposite direction, denied, or even betrayed their faith. Jesus still invites you and them to join him and take part in his Supper. His invitation is not conditional: "Do this, and then I'll do this for you."

Despite the disciples' flaws, Acts 4:13 also includes this: **"When they saw the courage of Peter and John . . . they** [the Sanhedrin] **were astonished and they took note that these men had been with Jesus."**

What made the disciples different? The company they kept was *with Jesus*. What makes you special is your Savior. Where can you go and worship him with fellow sinners who are now saints because they too are *with Jesus*? Your place at the heavenly banquet is set. Be assured of this as you join him for his Supper.

**April 19**

# Created for community
## Liz Schroeder

The idol of self-sufficiency is so common that we don't even notice it anymore. From Horatio Alger's "pull yourself up by your own bootstraps" mentality of the 19th century to the modern toddler's first sentence: "I do it self!," we adore and indulge our independence. At the same time, we experience poverty in broken relationships with God, with ourselves, and with others.

So which is it? Are we rugged individualists making it on our own steam, or are we beggars living lonely lives of quiet desperation?

**"Then God said, 'Let us make mankind in our image, in our likeness.' . . . So God created mankind in his own image, in the image of God he created them"** (Genesis 1:26,27).

The triune God of the Bible is no loner; Father, Son, and Holy Spirit exist in perfect community. He created us in his image, but ever since man's stage dive into rebellion, being known by another feels scary and vulnerable, a danger to be avoided rather than a goal to be pursued. Frankly, it's easier to be a hermit, safely insulated in a comfortable cave. But you're not a rock or an island. You were made for more.

Start by understanding that your relationship with God has been repaired through the work of Jesus. Your right relationship with God is foundational for restoring your knowledge of self. Finally, enjoy communion with your fellow followers of Christ—at the Lord's Supper on Sundays and on random weeknights as you break bread in each other's homes. It's what you were designed to do.

Easter Sunday | **April 20**

## Battle scars
Ann Jahns

On the palm of my right hand is a jagged, decades-old scar. My memory is a little fuzzy, but I seem to remember carrying a glass bottle to the garbage can in the garage—while on roller skates. I fell, and then . . . well, I think you can guess how that story ends.

The scars that mar our bodies are a testament to life in a broken world. We bear scars from illness and injury, from accidents, from abuse. Some of us carry "battle scars" earned on behalf of others.

After Jesus died, his distraught disciples locked themselves away in a house, paralyzed with fear. When the resurrected Jesus suddenly appeared to them, he needed a tangible way to prove that he was real and not a ghostly apparition. He said to his friends: **"'Touch me and see; a ghost does not have flesh and bones, as you see I have.' When he had said this, he showed them his hands and feet"** (Luke 24:39,40).

Eight days later, Jesus invited his skeptical friend Thomas to touch his scars to feel the evidence of his love: **"Put your finger here; see my hands,"** Jesus said. **"Reach out your hand and put it into my side. Stop doubting and believe"** (John 20:27).

How remarkable that Jesus' resurrected body still bore scars! He didn't hide them but shared them readily as visible reminders of the bottomless depth of his love for you and for me.

These have to be the most beautiful battle scars the world has ever seen.

**April 21**

# A new day of hope
## Clark Schultz

Early in my ministry as I was struggling as a single pastor in a mission church, a wise pastor told me, "Clark, get a good night's sleep. In the morning the bitterness of this day won't taste as bitter." Thinking him crazy, off to bed I went. The next day came. Yes, the hurt from the day before was still there, but I felt better with the hope of a new day ahead.

On Easter Sunday morning, what were the Marys thinking? **"After the Sabbath, at dawn on the first day of the week, Mary Magdalene and the other Mary went to look at the tomb"** (Matthew 28:1). When they had last seen their friend, his body was battered, bruised, and very much dead. This feeling of loss left them feeling bitter and without hope as they crept in the dark to the tomb. As the new day arrived and the sun rose, they soon knew the "SONrise." Their bitterness was turned to joy, wonder, excitement, and pure happiness because JESUS LIVES!

What bitterness are you tasting now? The empty tomb at dawn gives you the brightest picture that this life is not all there is. Each day is a fresh start. You can rejoice each day in the many reasons God gives you hope until he takes you home!

**April 22**

## What angels teach us about us
Mike Novotny

On Easter morning, as an angel waited to tell the women about the risen Jesus, Matthew tells us, **"The guards were so afraid of** [the angel] **that they shook and became like dead men"** (28:4). The guards—plural, Roman, trained, weapon-wielding—were so afraid of him—singular, alone—that they nearly died from the trauma.

What does this detail teach you? That standing in the presence of holiness will kill you. You might be a relatively good person or emotionally stronger than most people you know, but in the presence of one holy angel, you will melt with fear. And if that is true of an angel, imagine standing in the presence of God! He is the Most Holy One who prompts armies of angels to cry out, "Holy! Holy! Holy!" In other words, no one, no matter how confident they feel, will feel that way in the presence of holiness.

But don't panic just yet. Because the Easter story is filled with unholy people—Mary Magdalene, Peter, Thomas—being invited into the holy presence of Jesus. Yes, they panicked at first, but after Jesus calmed them with, "Do not fear," he showed them his holy wounds and reminded them of the peace that he had won for them that very weekend.

Easter reminds you what the rest of the Scriptures has already taught you—No one is worthy of God, but through the sacrifice of Jesus, there is hope. You can stand before his glorious presence with the angels themselves and cry out, "Holy! Holy! Holy!"

April 23

# He shall reign forever!
Dave Scharf

It's easy to look at our world with its tornadoes and flooding and inflation and disease and crime and wars and think, "Is God here? Is he really in control? Is he really the one who reigns over all things for my good?" God is the One who controls history. He revealed to Daniel the kingdoms to come, and then he revealed one final kingdom to rule them all: his own. Daniel 2:44 says, **"In the time of those kings, the God of heaven will set up a kingdom that will never be destroyed, nor will it be left to another people. It will crush all those kingdoms and bring them to an end, but it will itself endure forever."**

When the time was right, God sent *the* King. The angels sang when that King was born, and the shepherds worshiped in wonder. Our King, Jesus, saved this sinful world by dying for it on a cross. Three days later, King Jesus firmly established his rule by springing to life on Easter. He then ascended to heaven to reign over all things in heaven and on earth for the good of his church . . . for you. Ten days later, he firmly established his kingdom at Pentecost through the good news of the gospel. To this day and to the end of time, the gates of hell will not prevail against his kingdom. Jesus is here. He is in control. And he shall reign for ever and ever!

April 24

## Your Mediator
Nathan Nass

A man named Job in the Bible needed a mediator. Not for a court case. He needed a mediator between him and God. Listen to Job describe it: **"If only there were someone to mediate between us, someone to bring us together, someone to remove God's rod from me, so that his terror would frighten me no more"** (Job 9:33,34). It felt like God was his enemy. Job needed a mediator.

You and I do too. Who are we to approach God? We're mortal. God is immortal. We're sinful. God is perfectly holy. We are weak and frail. God is almighty. Who will mediate between us and God?

Jesus. That's exactly what Jesus came to do. **"There is one God and one mediator between God and mankind, the man Christ Jesus, who gave himself as a ransom for all people"** (1 Timothy 2:5,6). When our sins separated us from God, when our guilt earned God's punishment, Jesus came.

But Jesus did what no other mediator has ever done. He *"gave himself as a ransom for all people."* Jesus died on a cross to remove the sin that separated us from God. Jesus died on a cross to suffer the punishment from God that we deserved. Jesus saved us!

You have a Mediator—Jesus! When you sin, go to Jesus: "Thank you for dying for me!" When it seems like God is against you, go to Jesus and hear him say, "It's all taken care of!" Jesus is your Mediator.

# April 25

## Sing and feast on Jesus' victory!
Dave Scharf

Do you feel like singing today? Living in this life, we get used to living with disappointment, don't we? It's like there's a burial cloth over our lives and a layer of dust and ashes over everything we try to make prosper. But listen to what Jesus offers instead: **"The Lord Almighty will prepare a feast of rich food for all peoples, a banquet of aged wine—the best of meats and the finest of wines. . . . He will destroy the shroud that enfolds all peoples. . . . He will swallow up death forever"** (Isaiah 25:6-8).

Death swallowed up forever? How? One word: *Easter*. Have you ever noticed that Jesus "ruined" every funeral he went to? He touched a coffin in Nain, and that coffin was forced to cough up its contents. He stood at the tomb of his friend and simply said, "Come out." And do you know why Lazarus came out of the tomb? Because Jesus told him to. Death had met its match.

That's why in Isaiah 25, God describes a party where the shroud of death is gone, and only the finest wine and best meats are served. It's a party where everyone is singing about God's salvation. When will this happen? On the Last Day, but the victory has already been won. The party has already started. Jesus lays a feast before you as he allows you to chew on his promises for now and for eternity. So sing and feast on Jesus' victory!

April 26

## Words matter
Jan Gompper

Remember learning this phrase? *Sticks and stones may break your bones, but words will never hurt you.* Really? I don't know about you, but I've had physical injuries that healed much more readily than some of the verbal wounds I've experienced. Sadly, I've also inflicted some verbal wounds.

For the record—words matter. Don't take my word for it; look at what God has to say:

- Words have influence: **"The tongue has the power of life and death"** (Proverbs 18:21).
- Words can promote reconciliation or escalate tensions: **"A gentle answer turns away wrath, but a harsh word stirs up anger"** (Proverbs 15:1).
- Words can create lasting pain or lasting healing: **"The words of the reckless pierce like swords, but the tongue of the wise brings healing"** (Proverbs 12:18).
- Words mirror what's in our hearts: **"For the mouth speaks what the heart is full of. A good man brings good things out of the good stored up in him, and an evil man brings evil things out of the evil stored up in him"** (Matthew 12:34,35).
- Words have consequences: **"But I tell you that everyone will have to give account on the day of judgment for every empty word they have spoken. For by your words you will be acquitted, and by your words you will be condemned"** (Matthew 12:36,37).

In our politically, racially, and spiritually divided world, it's important to listen closely to the words people speak.

# See his hands
Liz Schroeder

Before you get a tattoo on the palm of your hand, you should know that it has 17,000 touch receptors and free nerve endings, making it one of the most painful places to pen. Even body ink aficionados with high thresholds of pain say no to imprinting their palms.

As the Son of God, Jesus would have known just how many pain receptors are in a human hand. The nails driven into his hands were just a drop in the cup of suffering he prayed to be taken from him, the cup he would drink on a cross.

Even after Jesus rose from the dead, his body still bore the marks of the nails and spear. **"Then he [Jesus] said to Thomas, 'Put your finger here; see my hands. Reach out your hand and put it into my side. Stop doubting and believe'"** (John 20:27). Do you doubt that Jesus has power over death? Do you question his love for you? Do you wonder if he has forgotten about you and your struggles?

**"Can a mother forget the baby at her breast and have no compassion on the child she has borne? Though she may forget, I will not forget you! See, I have engraved you on the palms of my hands"** (Isaiah 49:15,16).

I've never met a mom who regrets the pain she went through to give birth to her child. Jesus does not regret the pain he went through to make you his own. He can't forget you; you're engraved on his hands.

**April 28**

## God's steadfast love endures forever
Andrea Delwiche

Twenty-six times. That's how many times this phrase is repeated in Psalm 136: **"His steadfast love endures forever"** (ESV). I'm guilty of mindless mumbling when reading it aloud in church or skimming rather than digesting when reading. *"His steadfast love endures forever."* My "hurry up" mentality and thrill-seeking self both struggle to meander along a path of thanks.

Then another person read it to me with quiet music playing. Their deliberate pace kept me from racing along as the psalmist led me along the path of God's measurable, rock-steady love.

I found myself picturing some of the "great wonders" I saw on a recent road trip. *"His steadfast love endures forever."* I thought about the beautiful moonrise over Lake Michigan that I witnessed a few weeks ago. *"His steadfast love endures forever."* With the psalmist, I followed the Israelites' journey across the desert. I thought about the many ways God has protected and led me through my own life. *"His steadfast love endures forever."* The measured cadence of the refrain gave time for my distraction to dissipate. I settled into the goodness of God.

How could you adopt this psalm as your own personal psalm of praise? Where would you begin? Are there signs of God's steadfast love that surprise you?

Ask the Holy Spirit to help you settle in and ground yourself in a posture of attention and praise. How are God's provisions of old mirrored in your own life? The psalm's repetition can help you methodically prove it true: God's steadfast love endures forever.

April 29

## Which color of crayon are you?
Daron Lindemann

I remember as a kid having only two crayons to choose from for skin color: peach for white-skinned Caucasians like me or brown for everyone else.

Today you'll find a few more selections. Even better, a woman named Sabine Joseph has developed a new crayon color line that celebrates the beauty of all skin tones. Her crayons are intended to celebrate the diversity of skin colors in our world and to teach children that every ethnicity matters. God agrees.

God once sent a dream to the apostle Peter with all kinds of different foods. He told Peter to eat these different kinds of foods, some of which Peter had never eaten before because they were unclean.

Peter proclaimed, **"God has shown me that I should not call anyone impure or unclean"** (Acts 10:28).

In our prideful hearts, we quickly and often think of other ethnic groups as inferior. God will not have it. **"God does not show favoritism but accepts from every nation the one who fears him and does what is right"** (Acts 10:34,35).

As a man, Jesus' ethnicity is Jewish. As God, he has no ethnicity other than Savior of all people. Be sure that all the different people in your life know what you believe about Jesus and about them: **"Everyone who believes in him receives forgiveness of sins through his name"** (Acts 10:43).

*Teach me, Lord, to see other people for who they are and who you have made them to be. Amen.*

**April 30**

## Jesus shows up early
Mike Novotny

One of my favorite parts of the Easter story is how Jesus shows up early. As you read Matthew 28, you might assume that the women and the apostles would have to wait until Galilee to see Jesus, but then Jesus shows up early.

The angel said, **"'He . . . is going ahead of you into Galilee. There you will see him.' . . . So the women hurried away from the tomb, afraid yet filled with joy, and ran to tell his disciples. Suddenly Jesus met them"** (Matthew 28:7-9).

I love that. You and I will see Jesus one day in heaven, but apparently he likes to show up early! That is why he promised, **"Surely I am with you always"** (Matthew 28:20).

This means when you lay your head down tonight, Jesus will be there. When you're trying to be patient with that customer or your kid, Jesus will be there. When you're grateful and feeling good, Jesus will be there. When you're freaking out and afraid, Jesus will be there. When the scan is clear or they schedule surgery, Jesus will be there. When you finally get debt free or are trying to figure out what to do, Jesus will be there. Jesus isn't in some grave from the past. He isn't just at the finish line of your future. He rose so he could be right here with you. What couldn't you do if God was alive and with you?

*What would happen if you remembered the resurrection?*

# MAY

Ask rain from the Lord in the season of the spring rain,
from the Lord who makes the storm clouds,
and he will give them showers of rain, to
everyone the vegetation in the field.

ZECHARIAH 10:1

May 1

## A more than satisfying ending
Jan Gompper

If you're like me, how a movie/TV series ends can make or break your overall viewing satisfaction. Many endings these days feel contrived or incomplete, as if the screenwriter got tired or bored with the story and quickly put a final period on it.

I think the reason so many Hollywood endings are unsatisfying is because, deep down, human beings are wired for completion. We want to feel a sense of "rightness" at the end. Add a dash of hope, and we walk away much more satisfied.

That's because God never intended for his story for us to have an ending. He created the perfect setting and placed two main characters (Adam and Eve) into the scene, fully fleshed out with the free will to live and rule eternally. There was just one caveat—they were forbidden to eat the fruit of just one tree (Genesis 2:17).

Enter Satan, and the plot thickened. Adam and Eve disobeyed their Master Scriptwriter and altered the story.

But God didn't leave them with a disappointing ending. Instead, he rewrote his story, giving it a new ending. **"From now on you** (Satan) **and the woman** (Eve) **will be enemies, as will your offspring and hers. You will strike his heel, but he** (Jesus) **will crush your head"** (Genesis 3:15 TLB).

This very first promise of God's plan to send a Redeemer (his own Son) to pay a very costly price for their disobedience (and ours), gives all who trust in God's revised story a complete and hope-filled ending.

**"It is finished"** (John 19:30).

**May 2**

## Similar or sanctified?
Mike Novotny

One of the bigger challenges of the Christian life is what Jesus called being **"in the world"** but not **"of the world"** (John 17:11,16). Because every time you step into this world—your school, your workplace, your circle of friends, your online community—there will be a strong temptation to blend in by believing and behaving like most everyone else. Often in life, we have to choose between being similar to the world or sanctified (set apart) from the world.

For example, your friends have a certain style of humor, which might be God-pleasing or might frequently cross the line. Your family has a certain way of thinking about men and women, about immigrants and the president, about alcohol and money, and their views are likely a combination of good and bad. But since no one you know wants to be judged and since you like to be liked, assimilation is an ever-present temptation. Can you think of a situation in which you've felt significant pressure to sin similarly to your peers?

This is why Jesus not only died for our sins but also prayed for our sanctification. **"Sanctify them by the truth; your word is truth"** (John 17:17). Jesus wants you to be set apart from this world by your Word-based mindset and lifestyle.

The next time you find yourself under the pressure of your peers, silently repeat Jesus' prayer for yourself: "Father, sanctify me by the truth!"

## Greatest moment
C.L. Whiteside

What would you consider the greatest moment of your life? The usual responses deal with weddings, birthdays, childhood dreams fulfilled, and major feats accomplished. As a basketball coach at a Christian high school, my fellow coaches and players were faced with this question after capping off an undefeated season, being considered the undisputed best team in the state and greatest team in school history, and crushing an opponent in the state championship that had our number for the last three years.

After the season pinnacle of winning a championship, we reminded our players: "Don't let this be the greatest moment of your life." Why would we say this? Because as believers in Jesus, our greatest moment was even greater than a state championship: **"So in Christ Jesus you are all children of God through faith. Because you are his sons, God sent the Spirit of his Son into our hearts, the Spirit who calls out, 'Abba, Father.' So you are no longer a slave, but God's child; and since you are his child, God has made you also an heir"** (Galatians 3:26; 4:6,7).

Our greatest moment was when we were adopted into the family of believers and declared righteous and perfect through faith in Jesus Christ. Thankfully, our God allows and blesses us to have some dreamlike, incredible moments. But never forget your greatest moment was when the Spirit created faith in your heart and claimed you as God's child.

**May 4**

# Where the real power comes from
## Mike Novotny

In his classic text on spiritual warfare, Paul urges us to **"be strong in the Lord and in his mighty power"** (Ephesians 6:10). When temptation hits, there is a massive difference between you being strong and you being strong "in the Lord."

The former is when you search inside yourself for strength, when you get self-esteemy and say, "I am strong. I am enough. I got this." As common as that practice is, it leaves you with far too little strength, because true strength doesn't come from within.

Let me prove it. Did you know that the real power of a boxing punch (or the real oomph behind a home run swing) does not come from the chiseled physiques of professional athletes? They might have shoulders like cantaloupes, but that's not where their power comes from. The real force comes from . . . the ground! The power starts from the earth's stability and strength, which gets launched as kinetic energy through the body—first legs, then hips, then core, then BAM! Take a boxer, float him in the air, and his punch will lose almost all its power. But once you set his feet firmly on the earth, he'll have a source of super strength.

When you fight your spiritual battles, don't look inside yourself and think there's enough strength to stand up to Satan. Instead, grab your Bible, hit your knees in prayer, look to the cross, and plant the feet of your faith on something outside of yourself—the Rock that is our God. Be strong in the Lord!

May 5

## The walking, talking billboard
Ann Jahns

I drove past a puzzling billboard on the freeway. On a backdrop of a sunset sky with clouds were the large words "Jesus Christ." "Hope," "truth," and "love" were printed underneath. There was no context or contact information, and contrary to all marketing principles, no call to action. I wonder how effective this billboard is in encouraging its viewers to learn more about the work of Jesus.

Much more effective, I think, are those of us who believe in Jesus. We are walking, talking billboards for Christ. Because God's Spirit lives in us, we are compelled to talk, act, live, and love differently. We want the world to ask, "Why is there something different about you?"

First Peter 3:15 urges us: **"In your hearts revere Christ as Lord. Always be prepared to give an answer to everyone who asks you to give the reason for the hope that you have. But do this with gentleness and respect."**

The way we talk and work and live is a reflection of our Savior. A freeway billboard may get some disinterested passing glances before it gets papered over, but think how many meaningful interactions we will have with others in a lifetime.

Why are those who love Jesus different? We're different because Christ, our Savior, lives in us. We live differently because we have been redeemed by his blood.

*Dear Jesus, please give us the strength and courage to be walking, talking billboards who reflect your love and share the hope that we have in you! Amen.*

**May 6**

## It's a big deal
Dave Scharf

Are you sometimes tempted to think that what you do doesn't matter? Day-to-day life can seem monotonous and not worth anyone's attention. There are important people in the world . . . and then there's you and me. Jesus said, **"Truly I tell you, anyone who gives you a cup of water in my name because you belong to the Messiah will certainly not lose his reward"** (Mark 9:41).

I have a friend who's a hardworking and excellent plumber. He once drove six hours and did some significant plumbing work on my house. I thanked him profusely, but he looked at me and humbly said, "Pastor, what I do is nothing compared to what you do. My work isn't important." I thought, "Tell that to my wife! She now has a dishwasher!"

Martin Luther King Jr. once said, "If it falls your lot to be a street sweeper, sweep streets like Michelangelo painted pictures, sweep streets like Beethoven composed music."* Much of our lives of service is hidden from others but not from Jesus. The One who loved you so much that he came into this world to live for you, die for you, and rise for you loves to see you live for him. Even if no one does, Jesus sees and will remember, even if it's just a cup of water given to a thirsty person.

---

\* Martin Luther King Jr., "What Is Your Life's Blueprint?" (speech, Barratt Junior High School, Philadelphia, October 26, 1967), *The Seattle Times*, https://projects.seattletimes.com/mlk/words-blueprint.html.

May 7

## Never alone
### Clark Schultz

One hundred sixty is not the number of times my wife reminds me of what she just told me to pick up at the store. One hundred sixty may be the weight I clocked in at in my teens and wish I could weigh again. But one hundred sixty *is* the number of times the word *darkness* is referenced in the Bible.

In many places, the darkness is a negative, such as Matthew 8:12: **"The darkness, where there will be weeping and gnashing of teeth."** While that's uncomfortable for unbelievers, there is comfort or light for believers in the darkness: **"*Darkness* was over the surface of the deep"** (Genesis 1:2). At creation there was darkness, but there was and is God's Spirit hovering over the water. The darkness in Exodus 10:21 **("*darkness* that can be felt")** made the Egyptians feel uncomfortable, but the people of Israel were in the light because God was with them.

As the disciples battled the wind and the waves before dawn, Jesus was there to calm their fears (Matthew 14:25). And when the ultimate darkness was felt on the cross in Mark 15:33 **("At noon, *darkness* came over the whole land")**, when God turned his back on his Son, it meant we now have God's acceptance and assurance that no matter how dark our days seem, God will never turn his back on us.

**"On those living in the land of deep darkness a light has dawned"** (Isaiah 9:2). Light or dark, we are NEVER alone.

May 8

## Not all heroes wear capes
Jan Gompper

Did you have a childhood hero? Superman? Batman? Wonder Woman? Some other caped crusader? If you had a biblical upbringing, people like David (who slew Goliath) or Moses (who led the Israelites out of Egypt) may come to mind.

Heroes are often people with extraordinary powers who can see and do things mere mortals cannot, such as leap tall buildings in a single bound. Or they may be people who have risked their own lives for the sake of others.

As I've matured, my definition of what a hero is has changed. One of my heroes today is my 97-year-old aunt. Aunt Betty lost her husband to a stroke when she was in her 50s. She never remarried, nor did I ever hear her blame God or bemoan her loss. Her positive outlook and infectious laugh still inspire me.

Another more recent hero is a woman in our church named Paula. Despite numerous foot surgeries that require her to use a scooter most days, she still oversees the resale store (which she initially spearheaded) to help support the food bank at our church that feeds over five hundred economically challenged people every week.

And then there are all the widows, widowers, and other seniors who stand in the hot Florida sun each week to package and distribute the food for the food bank.

My heroes today don't wear capes. They are heroes because they **"act justly . . . love mercy . . . walk humbly with** [their] **God"** (Micah 6:8).

May 9

## The target audience
Jason Nelson

Someday, curious students in an advanced history or sociology class will study the first quarter of the 21st century. They will be able to analyze the times accurately because there will be a digital record of everything. I predict they will shake their heads in disbelief and ask, "How did it get that way? How did so many good people in a great country become extreme in their political and cultural views?"

By then, the passing of time will provide some clarity, and the effects will be self-evident. But understanding the causes will be the grist for doctoral research. They will discover that one target audience for extreme movements is often single and isolated young men, and it has been throughout history because they are vulnerable for recruitment to conspiracies' violence.

I'll let you gather with friends in your discussion group and identify radicals and terrorists that illustrate my point. I want to move on to my counterpoint and hopefully leave you wondering about it. It was precisely that audience that Jesus targeted to be his first disciples. He said to them, **"Whoever wants to be my disciple must deny themselves and take up their cross and follow me"** (Matthew 16:24). They followed him because they had very little to lose. They are saints to us now, but they didn't start out that way.

Next time you're in church, look around and ask yourself, "Where are the single young men?"

**May 10**

## Encourage one another
Nathan Nass

It's hard to give yourself an actual pat on the back. Have you ever noticed that? I suppose there are people who are flexible enough to pat their backs with their hands. For most of us, however, it's hard to reach. Someone else has to do that for us.

That's the way God set up the world. The Bible encourages Christians to **"not give up meeting together, as some are in the habit of doing, but encourage one another—and all the more as you see the Day approaching"** (Hebrews 10:25). We need to encourage one another as judgment day approaches.

People like to say that their faith is just between them and God. That's a selfish thought, and it's not what the Bible says. We can't do it alone. We need other Christians to encourage us in our faith. And other Christians need us to encourage them in their faith. If you've gotten in the habit of not meeting with other Christians, you're hurting yourself and sinning against others.

You can't give yourself a pat on the back, so God has put other Christians in your life to encourage you and point you to Jesus. And all those other Christians can't give themselves a pat on the back either, so God gives you opportunities to encourage them and point them to Jesus. To whom could you give a pat on the back today? We all need it, don't we? Encourage one another!

Mother's Day | **May 11**

## Jesus & Moms
Nate Wordell

This year, Mother's Day falls on Good Shepherd Sunday, which is perfect. Jesus cares for little lambs through mothers.

My mom was a professional snack dispenser. She provided for me—just like Jesus. **"The Lord is my shepherd; I shall not want."**

Mom didn't give me everything I wanted but always what I needed—just like Jesus. **"He makes me lie down in green pastures. He leads me beside still waters."**

Mom refreshed my soul. When I was a rascal, she said, "I forgive you"—just like Jesus. **"He restores my soul."**

When I wanted to do something stupid, she showed me right from wrong—just like Jesus. **"He leads me in paths of righteousness for his name's sake."**

When I left the nest, I walked through some dark valleys. But my mom taught me that my Good Shepherd is always with me. **"Even though I walk through the valley of the shadow of death . . . you are with me; your rod and your staff, they comfort me."**

My brave mother shows me that there is no enemy so great, no cancer so pervasive, no relationship so frayed that it scares our Savior. **"You prepare a table before me in the presence of my enemies."**

Moms chase kids everywhere, and Jesus is still after them and you. **"Surely goodness and mercy shall follow me all the days of my life."**

Jesus lives so that Christian moms and all their babies can live together forever. **"I shall dwell in the house of the Lord forever"** (Psalm 23 ESV).

*May 12*

# With no doubts
## Linda Buxa

Peter, a disciple of Jesus, was known for his boldness—stepping out of a boat and walking on water; cutting off a soldier's ear; telling Jesus, "Never!"

After Jesus died, rose, and went back to heaven, Peter was still known for his boldness with keeping Jewish laws and customs. Then one day he received visions that changed his whole attitude. Instead of telling Jews that the Messiah had come, he was being sent to Gentiles, people normally considered "unclean." The Holy Spirit told him, **"Get up, go downstairs, and go with them with no doubts at all, because I have sent them"** (Acts 10:20 CSB).

Boy, do I need the reminder to act "with no doubts at all." I hear of opportunities to serve, but I wrestle with doing the good works God prepared for me to do. He says he'll be with me. But sometimes out of fear I question that. The Lord tells me he works all things for good. I've seen it in the past, yet I'm tempted to doubt he'll do it in the future. He says he will provide, but do I really believe that with no doubts at all? The God of the universe invites me to pray boldly, and then I ask timidly because I doubt if he really is going to do what I ask.

What is God calling you to do that gives you pause? Won't you join me in getting up and fulfilling that purpose—with no doubts at all?

**May 13**

# Tank Man and our courageous Jesus
Mike Novotny

On June 4, 1989, a group of Chinese students gathered to protest in Beijing's Tiananmen Square, a day now famous for the massacre that ensued. Troops and students clashed, and hundreds, if not thousands, were machine-gunned down and crushed by tanks. The following day, a line of 18 tanks rolled down the empty ten-laned Avenue of Eternal Peace as a show of government dominance. That's when Tank Man appeared.

No one knows his name, who he was, or where he came from, but a man stepped alone into the middle of the road, plastic shopping bag in his hand. He stood in front of the first tank, a tiny man in front of a war machine, and did not move. When the tank tried to swerve around him, Tank Man moved too, standing his ground, stopping all 18 tanks in their tracks. The image taken that day, now considered one of the most iconic photographs of all time, is a striking picture of resolve.

Jesus was like that. Luke chapter 9 says, **"As the time approached for him to be taken up to heaven, Jesus resolutely set out for Jerusalem"** (verse 51). Jesus was so committed to saving you and me, to being crushed by the tank of the cross and to conquering the grave, that he resolved to finish the mission of his heavenly Father. The Greek of this verse says, "Jesus fixed his face to go to Jerusalem." He was that committed to our salvation.

It took courage for Jesus to save us. Take a moment today to praise our courageous Savior!

**May 14**

## Who's next?
Jon Enter

Do you think the Old Testament believers instantly understood that the prophet Micah was prophesying the exact location of the Savior's birth? **"But you, Bethlehem Ephrathah, though you are small among the clans of Judah, out of you will come for me one who will be ruler over Israel, whose origins are from of old, from ancient times"** (Micah 5:2).

This was hard for the Israelites to understand. Bethlehem was a small, nowhere town of a conquered people. Why not have the Savior be born in Jerusalem, the capital city, where David once made the Israelites feared and famous?

This prophecy fulfilled in Jesus' humble birth shows who God is. The Lord loves to use meek things to do the magnificent. He chose an unwed teenager to be the Savior's mother. He gathered 12 mismatched, unsavory characters to be his disciples. He chose death on a cross to bring us spiritual life.

God still does the same. He makes you and me his messengers. Flawed as we are, he gives power to our proclamations of his love. He uses water and the Word in Baptism, so simple, to start or strengthen saving faith. Bread and wine, simple food and drink, are connected to his true body and blood to forgive eternally.

God does the incredible with the ordinary. Don't downplay what God and his almighty power can do through your simple prayers to him. Praying for someone is one of the most meaningful and mighty things you can do. Who can you pray for next?

**May 15**

# God has mighty power
Mike Novotny

When you are battling temptations, Paul tells you to **"be strong in the Lord and in his mighty power"** (Ephesians 6:10).

The apostle uses two Greek words to form the phrase "mighty power." The first is *kratos*—the power to control things. The second is *ischus*—the ability to do something effectively. They mean you have a God who's in total control of your life and uses everything effectively for your good. That belief is a weapon in this spiritual war!

Let's say you're trying not to worry about money. You could try to "be strong" in your own ability to control your finances: "I'm going to get that promotion, start that business." As noble as your intentions might be, however, you lack both the *kratos* and the *ischus* to guarantee a good result. You lack the power to control the economy or the accident that leaves you with unexpected insurance bills. Look in the mirror, and you'll have plenty to worry about.

But be strong "in the Lord and in his mighty power" and you deal your worry a deadly blow. "My Father has the power and the ability to provide for me. He will work all things for my good and keep his promise to give me my daily bread. If he didn't spare his own Son when I was just a sinner, how could he not take care of me now that I'm his child?"

Whatever your spiritual struggle, consider what it looks like to find your strength not in yourself but in the Lord's mighty power.

**May 16**

## God's battle in Jericho
Daron Lindemann

The battle of Jericho is an epic Bible account of faith and victory. Skeptics say it's merely a folktale. Christians say it's true. Archaeological discoveries confirm it.

The Bible records the event in Joshua 6. The walls of Jericho collapsed when God's followers marched around the city, worshiped, and shouted.

Historically, when a city's wall was breached, either an army used a battering ram to break the wall inward or built a ramp for soldiers to climb up and over the wall. Neither happened at Jericho. Archaeological digs have discovered that the wall crumbled on top of itself and then tumbled—outward! That allowed God's army immediate access. Here's exactly what the Bible says: **"The wall collapsed; so everyone charged straight in, and they took the city"** (Joshua 6:20).

The citizens of Jericho were well prepared for the siege that preceded this charge. They had dug a fresh well and filled their storage containers with food. Guess what archaeologists have found? Lots of large jars in Jericho homes—full of grain. Also, charred evidence of a sudden fire.

Here's exactly what the Bible says happened after God's army marched in through the crumbled wall: **"They burned the whole city and everything in it"** (Joshua 6:24).

Normally, conquered cities like Jericho were depleted of food, either by the siege or from the victorious army taking it. But not Jericho. God didn't need the plunder of Jericho. God wanted everything burned for a fresh new start . . . with him in charge.

**May 17**

## Feeling guilty?
Jon Enter

What do you feel guilty about? What have you done that haunts you? When that memory comes to mind, it often makes you feel awful. You've got guilt. We all do. And left unchecked, guilt crushes.

Today's verse is one to memorize to calm your troubled conscience and make guilt go away! It's Psalm 103:10: **"He does not treat us as our sins deserve or repay us according to our iniquities."** God doesn't go after you to teach you a lesson; God goes after you to bring you back to him. He doesn't treat you as you deserve.

When you feel guilty, that means there's fear of the punishment you deserve. But Jesus took on your punishment. The price is paid! That sin is gone! The punishment is over! God doesn't repay you according to what you've done. God treats you according to what Jesus has done.

Would it make sense for me to punish my 15-year-old for something she did when she was 5? That would be terrible parenting! She wouldn't learn; she'd resent me. God doesn't stockpile your sins to punish you later. He piled them on the loving shoulders of Jesus and crucified their punishment on him.

Don't let the devil convince you to feel guilty over sins you've confessed to Jesus. They're gone! Don't focus on guilt; focus on grace, because that's what you have in Jesus!

You're loved. You're forgiven. You're freed from your sins. May the Lord lead you to trust that truth.

**May 18**

## It's not about me or you
### Liz Schroeder

"Some men brought to him a paralyzed man, lying on a mat. When Jesus saw their faith, he said to the man, 'Take heart, son; your sins are forgiven'" (Matthew 9:2).

Consider what would have happened if the paralytic man had said, "Don't make a fuss about me." When I say things like that, I think I'm being humble and selfless: "Prayer requests? Nah, I'm good. There are so many people who have it worse. Don't bother God with my little problems."

But it's not about me or you.

If the paralyzed man had said, "Don't make a fuss about me," we would have missed out on a rich lesson of forgiveness, of the Lord Jesus knowing what we truly need. I'm not sure the man had a plan beyond being plopped down at the feet of Jesus. None of the gospel writers records the man saying anything prior to the miracle of forgiveness and healing. But after Jesus healed him and told him to pick up his mat and go home, the man praised God on the way out the door.

If the paralyzed man had said, "Don't make a fuss about me," we would have missed out on a lesson about humility, what immediate obedience looks like, and a God-pleasing response to healing.

When you're in need of forgiveness and healing or when you don't even know what you need, let your friends make a fuss about you, taking you to the feet of Jesus. It's not about you.

**May 19**

# The end of B.C.
Mike Novotny

I can still remember my life B.C. (Before Community). It looked like a middle school me who believed in Jesus, went to church, and said his prayers but didn't have a true Christian community. Or the college me who still believed in Jesus, still read his Bible, and started giving 10% of his (puny) paychecks to church but still didn't have a community to confess sins to or be forgiven of sins by. I had Jesus in my heart, but I didn't have Jesus' people by my side.

Thank God my B.C. days are over. For over a decade now, I have tasted and seen that the Lord's people are good. As intimidating as honesty can be, I cannot imagine not being honest with them. Why did I go so long bearing my burdens alone? Why did I wait so long to allow God to heal and help me through the words and wisdom of his people? I don't know, but I do know that this is how the Christian life was always meant to be lived.

Do you have a community to confess your sins to? If so, thank God! If not, today is the day to end your B.C days and start a new era of your Christian life. You might be scared, even terrified, but God is waiting to bless you in ways you can't yet imagine. **"Carry each other's burdens, and in this way you will fulfill the law of Christ"** (Galatians 6:2).

**May 20**

# Some demons won't come out
Jason Nelson

Jesus has a reputation for being able to do miraculous things. **"Jesus healed many who had various diseases. He also drove out many demons"** (Mark 1:34). That creates expectations in the Christian community anytime illness strikes. We pray for a cure. To be sure, I believe in miracles. I have experienced miraculous healing myself through highly skilled agents of Jesus' power over sickness.

But mental illnesses are often stubbornly resistant to recoveries. They have reached epidemic levels in our society. We have become painfully aware of the role of mental illness in criminal behavior. Everyone is talking about it. No one knows what to do about it. Like many diseases, they can be treated but not cured. But mentally ill people need to ask for treatment themselves and comply with regimens of psychotropic medications. Most just won't do it. So "being off their meds" is a sad joke and leads to violent tragedies.

The demons Jesus drove out of people were unwilling participants in the process of healing. **"The demons begged Jesus, 'If you drive us out, send us into the herd of pigs'"** (Matthew 8:31). They pleaded for an alternative to what they knew they had coming. In the end, they had no choice.

We need to find the resolve to pray to God for help and to act in the best interest of mentally ill people who are incapable of advocating for themselves. It will be controversial. But if we can do it, even their demons won't separate them from the love of God.

**May 21**

# A pool of tears
Andrea Delwiche

Have you ever judged another person's anger? Have you wondered how someone pursues a line of reasoning or justification that you just can't understand? It's hard to step into another's shoes and empathize with their anger and passionate point of view.

Written during the time when God's people had been carried off to Babylon, Psalm 137 voices incredible grief. The last two verses are hard to read. Speaking to their captors, they cried: **"Daughter Babylon, doomed to destruction, happy is the one who repays you according to what you have done to us. Happy is the one who seizes your infants and dashes them against the rocks"** (verses 8,9).

After listening to this psalm, I realized I had missed previously that the psalmist is wishing upon the Babylonian parents the same suffering that Jewish families had experienced: "Happy is the one who seizes *your* infants." Does this psalm model forgiveness? No. Is it a raw cry of grief and suffering? Most definitely.

A 20th-century Christian leader spoke about the need to offer to others the grace *we* would like to receive. He memorably stated, "Everyone sits by their own pool of tears."

Psalm 137 is a telling of tears. It's important enough to be included in the pages of Scripture, ugly as it is. Is there someone whom you are judging for their reactions? Do you know what trauma filled their pool of tears? Ask the Spirit to help you pray and to hold space for another's grief and suffering.

**May 22**

## What have you lost?
Daron Lindemann

What do the following have in common? A fog machine. A pin with Jesus holding a slice of pizza. An ankle monitor. Some horns and a Viking helmet. A slab of bluefin tuna for sushi. And 16 ounces of fake blood.

All of these items have been lost by Uber riders.

What have you lost in your life? Maybe you lost your job, your friend, your health, the church family that was such a big part of your life, or a loved one who died. Maybe you lost your focus, your willpower, your virginity, your positivity, or the spark in your marriage.

People lose all kinds of things that really matter. Here's the good news: Jesus knows exactly where they are. All of them! Where?

In him. He holds all things, knows all things, and can give you all things. Get to know him better, and you will truly lose fewer things that are important to you. And besides, if Jesus knows where they are, then are they really lost? **"For I am the Lord your God who takes hold of your right hand and says to you, Do not fear; I will help you"** (Isaiah 41:13).

*Jesus, how can I lose anything when you know where to find it, how to replace it, or why I don't need it? You hold all things, even as you hold my life perfectly in your grace. Guide my searching to find what I need in you. Amen.*

**May 23**

## It's more than the name
C.L. Whiteside

When I say he's the greatest and his name is Michael, whom do you think of? You might think of the pop music icon. You might think of the basketball player or the swimmer or the actor. They are considered great because of what they did or do and based on how much influence they have on people. But having the common name of Michael doesn't automatically make them great.

There was another name a couple thousand years ago that was pretty common; the name was Jesus. But Jesus, the most famous person ever, obviously distinguished himself from other Jesuses. He was known as Jesus of Nazareth and eventually as Jesus Christ. Christ means "anointed one"; he was called this because he was chosen to be the promised Savior of the world.

Through his miracles, he proved that he was both man and God. Jesus did so many miracles that John 21:25 says there wasn't enough room to keep track of them all! What made Jesus so special and the most important person ever is made very clear in Acts 4:12: **"Salvation is found in no one else, for there is no other name under heaven given to mankind by which we must be saved."** We can't earn our own salvation and are only saved because of what Jesus did. Not only has Jesus done breathtaking miracles and lived a perfect life; he has paid the debt of every single person who existed or will exist. Jesus has loved like no other person can. He's the greatest, and it's not even close!

**May 24**

## The mudroom
Nathan Nass

Many houses have a mudroom. Do you know what I'm talking about? When you enter some houses through the garage or back door, there's a little room where people can take off their shoes before entering the house. Since it's filled with shoes, that mudroom is often the dirtiest and smelliest place in the house. You pass through it as quickly as possible to get to the real comforts of home.

Do you know what's like a mudroom? Earth. Your life on this earth. It's dirty and smelly. It's filled with sin and all the disappointment sin brings. It's often a mess. No matter how hard you try to clean it up, you can't ever keep it clean. Doesn't that sound like life on earth? It's like the mudroom in your house.

You haven't seen the rest of the house yet though. Do you know what's coming for you? Heaven! Eternal life with Jesus! You wouldn't want anyone to judge your house based on the mudroom. So don't judge life based on what you see here on earth. You're not seeing the whole story. Jesus didn't come to clean up the mudroom. He came to give you and me access to God's mansion in heaven by faith in Jesus.

**"So we fix our eyes not on what is seen, but on what is unseen, since what is seen is temporary, but what is unseen is eternal"** (2 Corinthians 4:18). Earth's mudroom is temporary. Heaven is eternal. Fix your eyes on heaven!

## I hope
Ann Jahns

The other day in a parking lot, I walked past a car from South Carolina. On its license plate was the state's motto: "While I breathe, I hope." A little research told me it's from the Latin phrase, *Dum spiro, spero*. It seems like an awfully biblical sentiment to be stamped into a metal license plate.

The concept of hope is woven throughout the pages of Scripture. One of the most uplifting pictures of it is painted in Isaiah 40:31: **"But those who hope in the Lord will renew their strength. They will soar on wings like eagles; they will run and not grow weary, they will walk and not be faint."**

Hope is a beautiful thing, isn't it? Hope gives us the strength to fight during cancer treatment. Hope is infused in our fervent prayers for a straying loved one. Hope keeps us moving forward even when we don't think we possibly can.

But only having hope in things like medical technology, our own strength, or our relationships isn't enough. All those can fail. Only hope anchored in Christ will never fail.

But as beautiful as hope is, we won't need it forever, will we? It's bound to this earth. If hope is the intense yearning for something we don't yet have, we will no longer need hope when we are in the presence of Jesus in heaven. All our hope will finally be fulfilled in him.

But for now, while you breathe, keep hoping. Take strength in the hope you have in Jesus!

May 26

## Praying with thanksgiving
Nate Wordell

Commonsense peace comes after you get what you want. It makes sense to have peace after you get your dream job, meet a special someone, or see how things worked out. But how do you have peace before that?

The apostle Paul recommends prayer with thanksgiving: **"Do not be anxious about anything, but in every situation, by prayer and petition, with thanksgiving, present your requests to God"** (Philippians 4:6).

A normal understanding is to give thanks after you get what you ask for. You certainly can thank God for the good things he puts in your life. But this passage says you don't just receive gifts with thanksgiving; you present your requests with thanksgiving. Thank God when you ask for a new job. Thank God when you're waiting for a happy ending. Give thanks even as you are asking.

How can you thank God for something when you don't even know what he's going to give you? The only way is if you trust he will bless you no matter how he answers your prayer. If God gives you what you ask, it will be good. If he says no, it will also be good. You can thank God ahead of time for all the possible ways he might answer your prayer—because you trust him.

This is not the peace of common sense. It's the peace of faith that only comes from God.

**"And the peace of God, which transcends all understanding, will guard your hearts and your minds in Christ Jesus"** (Philippians 4:7).

**May 27**

## God's answer to evil
Dave Scharf

Sometimes I'm shocked by the evil out there. Then I think about how evil is not just "out there" but in my heart too. What's the answer to evil? God gives us his answer in Psalm 90:13,14: **"Have compassion on your servants. Satisfy us in the morning with your unfailing love, that we may sing for joy and be glad all our days."**

God loves us. We may ask, "Where is God when evil things are happening?" God has an answer for that. His answer is Jesus. In Jesus, God becomes us. From everlasting to everlasting, God is God—no beginning, no end. But he still chose to dwell in the womb of the virgin Mary. He stepped out of eternity into this suffering world to be near us. He saw our hurt, and he wanted to take it away. That's compassion. God couldn't just teach us how to be better or less evil because our hearts wouldn't be any less sinful. So Jesus had to die for our sins. God judged Jesus guilty so he can now judge us innocent.

As hard as it is, God allows sin to continue on this earth right up until the moment when judgment comes . . . because he wants us to hear about his forgiveness and live. That's unfailing love. That means there's no hell for our secret sins, no punishment for our evil. Forgiveness is God's answer to evil.

**May 28**

## Two are better than one
Linda Buxa

I work at a high school, and one of the highlights of homecoming week is dodgeball. The game is intense, and the crowd's cheers are deafening. This year, the seniors' team had been whittled down until one sweet girl found herself outnumbered, one against seven.

The balls were flying around her head and her body, and she was ducking and dodging, so overwhelmed and stressed. Then, almost miraculously, she caught a ball. This meant one teammate could rejoin the playing field. Her relief was palpable when she saw a friend coming out to help her take on the much larger crowd.

Maybe you feel like that, outnumbered by the challenges you are facing. The bills are flying at your head. The bad news hits your gut. The family tension is overwhelming. The pressure to balance school or work with relationships and volunteering and rest is stressful. And then you have a friend who comes along and is willing to stand alongside you in your battle. Someone who steps up to remind you that you aren't alone and that **"two are better than one, because they have a good return for their labor: If either of them falls down, one can help the other up. But pity anyone who falls and has no one to help them up"** (Ecclesiastes 4:9,10).

This verse is also a reminder that even if the people around you let you down, your Savior—who fought alone on a cross on your behalf—has promised he will never leave you or forsake you.

**May 29**

# Three helps for being real with Jesus
Daron Lindemann

Federal agents trained to identify counterfeit money can't possibly be exposed to all counterfeit varieties. So instead, they learn what real money looks and feels like. Anything else is fake.

**"There will be false teachers among you,"** the Bible warns (2 Peter 2:1). False teachers are preachers or influencers, anyone who comments on social media or provides commentary on politics, and any video or show or podcast that claims to speak God's truth but does not.

The best way to identify false teachers is knowing what the real thing looks like. Be real with Jesus.

Here are three helps for being more real with Jesus.

1. **"Can I let Jesus see the real me?"** You can be guarded in some situations or with some people, and rightly so. But you need to be less guarded with Jesus. He can handle you. He loves and saved you.

2. **"Do I invite Jesus into my problems without telling him what to do?"** Jesus isn't limited, unless you limit him. Jesus is waiting to give you blessings. His way. Learn to yield and surrender to him, and watch what he can do.

3. **"Is Jesus so real in my life that others say, 'I want what you have'?"** People notice. They're hurting, and they're trying to find the good life. They see you secure in your salvation. Your words and actions give away your true identity in Christ.

That's real!

## Sometimes it's "Or"
### Jan Gompper

I would venture to guess that many of us often ask God to answer our prayers in a "do this" or "do that" fashion.

- "Lord, let me get the promotion at work. Or help me find a new job."
- "Lord, let my boyfriend propose to me. Or bring someone new into my life."

You probably know from experience that God doesn't necessarily answer either option we give him. Sometimes God's answers lie in the "Or."

The prophet Isaiah understood this when he wrote: **"For my thoughts are not your thoughts, neither are your ways my ways, declares the Lord. For as the heavens are higher than the earth, so are my ways higher than your ways and my thoughts than your thoughts"** (Isaiah 55:8,9 ESV).

Our prayers can try to box God in to *our* way of thinking. We often desire a quick-fix solution to an issue or problem we're facing, but our loving Father may have something different or even better in store for us—something we can't imagine or foresee—something that draws us closer to him.

There's nothing wrong with praying for specific things, but we can also keep the prophet Jeremiah's words in mind: **"Call to me and I will answer you, and will tell you great and *hidden* things that you have not known"** (Jeremiah 33:3 ESV).

Sometimes God's answer is hidden in the "Or."

**May 31**

## Jesus never chose between grace and truth
Mike Novotny

Every eyewitness would agree that you couldn't put Jesus of Nazareth in a box. You couldn't categorize him as kind/compassionate/gentle *or* bold/direct/truthful, because he was always, every time he opened his mouth, both. Jesus would preach about heaven and hell, salvation and condemnation, your blessings and God's brimstone. Jesus stooped down to flip over tables in anger and bent down to pick up little children in love. Jesus got up in people's faces and got down to wash people's feet. Jesus didn't choose one or the other. Our Savior was full of grace *and* truth.

Look how his friend John described him: **"We have seen his glory, the glory of the one and only Son, who came from the Father, full of grace and truth"** (John 1:14). Jesus wasn't a moral Arnold Palmer drink, half lemonade love and half iced-tea truth. Nah. Jesus was all of them both, loving people unconditionally and preaching truth without apology. That's why he unapologetically calls you to repentance and unconditionally comforts you with his grace.

What would it look like for you to imitate Jesus today? What sharp edges would you need to sand down in order to imitate his gentleness? Which courageous conversations would you need to have to imitate his honesty? Your loved ones would love to find out. I bet the One full of grace and truth would too.

# JUNE

Forgive us our debts,
as we also have forgiven our debtors.

MATTHEW 6:12

**June 1**

## Who's in charge?
Jon Enter

Do you think the president is leading the nation well? How about your governor or mayor? There are great leaders and then . . . well, ones that challenge your patience and anger index. In the Bible, Zechariah recorded how God felt about the corrupt and inept leaders of Israel: **"My anger burns against the shepherds, and I will punish the leaders; for the Lord Almighty will care for his flock, the people of Judah, and make them like a proud horse in battle"** (Zechariah 10:3). When the leaders (called shepherds) of Israel didn't lead Israel properly, the Lord's anger burned.

God cares. God expects your leaders to lead you with respect and integrity. When they don't, God's anger burns. He's perfect and wants righteousness to reign. Yet God expects that you honor your leaders in how you talk about them. God expects that you support your leaders by praying for them, not against them. **"I urge, then, first of all, that petitions, prayers, intercession and thanksgiving be made for all people—for kings and all those in authority"** (1 Timothy 2:1,2).

Are you excited about the leaders in office? If the answer is yes, pray for them. If the answer is no, definitely pray for them.

Know this: Regardless of who leads you with their earthly power, the Lord leads you with his almighty power. Zechariah encourages us this way: "The Lord Almighty will care for his flock." You are safe in his care. And that truth, well, that changes everything.

June 2

## You weren't made to be liked
Nate Wordell

What do you want when you want attention? If you post something on social media and people click the thumbs-up, what is pleasurable about that? When you're around a table and your comment gets a laugh, what about that makes you smile? When you win some tiny tournament for attention online or at dinner, congratulations! You get a dopamine rush. But the terms and conditions of dopamine say that it won't last long. That's because you weren't made to be liked. You weren't made for attention. And I think we've all figured out by now that we were not made for social media.

When you were knit together in your mother's womb, as your body took shape and your brain developed, something secret was installed in your heart of hearts. There was placed at the center of your soul a longing for some exquisite and inexhaustible affection. Ecclesiastes 3:11 says that God **"set eternity in the human heart."** Haven't you felt it there? No matter how many likes you feed your heart, it's always hungry for more—more posts, more laughs, more recognition, more trophies. It's exhausting.

**"Come to me, all you who are weary and burdened, and I will give you rest"** (Matthew 11:28). St. Augustine said that the love of Jesus is like a well-loved child crawling into a father's lap. You don't need to perform for him or make him laugh. He loves you for who you are, just as you are. You have his attention, and *that's* what you were made for.

**June 3**

## 500 days in a cave
### Daron Lindemann

Extreme athlete Beatriz Flamini broke the record for number of days spent isolated in a cave—500 days! She described her experience as excellent and unbeatable.

Flamini entered the 230-foot deep cave at age 48 and came out when she was 50. She had spent her time exercising, drawing, and knitting hats. She read a total of 60 books and drank 1,000 liters of water. Who would volunteer for such solitary confinement?

Actually, we are all trying to hide from something.

In the Bible, Jonah tried to hide from God, who had called him to preach to Nineveh. He boarded a ship headed the opposite direction and then hid below deck. But God found him.

Actually, God knew where he was the whole time. Better than that, God was with him the whole time. **"'Who can hide in secret places so that I cannot see them?' declares the Lord. 'Do not I fill heaven and earth?'"** (Jeremiah 23:24).

It's as if God chased Jonah wherever he went. And that's good news.

You have a God who pursues you, seeks your soul, finds you when you're lost, watches you when you're lonely, guards you when you're afraid, and came all the way from heaven to die for you.

So stop hiding. Instead of running from God, run to God. **"The name of the Lord is a fortified tower; the righteous run to it and are safe"** (Proverbs 18:10).

**June 4**

## The upside of relapse
Liz Schroeder

Axel and Angel hit 90 days of sobriety, a milestone often accompanied by increased levels of energy and hopefulness. They also experienced increased levels of frustration and agitation because the sober-living home, which had felt like a haven of security and order, now felt like a cage.

So one Phoenix morning, they left. With no plan and little money, they found trouble quickly. After two nights on the street, they returned home, sunburned and broken.

**"But while he was still a long way off, his father saw him and was filled with compassion for him; he ran to his son, threw his arms around him and kissed him. 'For this son of mine was dead and is alive again; he was lost and is found'"** (Luke 15:20,24).

If you have returned to a sin you thought you had kicked, please know that relapse can be redeemed. A step backward in recovery can be a step forward in your pursuit of the God who is running to you.

The prodigal son's story in Luke 15 ends with a feast and a party. Axel and Angel's story is still being written. A few weeks after returning to the sober-living home, they left again. I saw them recently at a bus stop. I wanted to see how they were doing, but my youngest was in the car with me, and I try to maintain safe boundaries. Instead, we prayed to the compassionate Father for their safety and return. May they find in the church the arms of Jesus to hug and welcome them home.

**June 5**

## The gift of purpose
Andrea Delwiche

God has given each of us the gift of purpose. **"For though the Lord is high, he regards the lowly, but the haughty he knows from afar. The Lord will fulfill his purpose for me"** (Psalm 138:6,8 ESV).

What is God's purpose for us? By faith, God wants us to seek him, trust him, turn to him.

Each of us is also called in our own circumstances and according to our abilities to carry out the hallmarks of God's love: **"to do justice, and to love kindness, and to walk humbly with your God"** (Micah 6:8 ESV); **"to stir up one another to love and good works"** (Hebrews 10:24 ESV); to love one another (1 John); and to practice hospitality (Romans 12).

These may seem like unimpressive activities, but doing them will fill a lifetime and change many lives. Consider Jesus' words: **"You are the salt of the earth. . . . You are the light of the world"** (Matthew 5:13,14 ESV). **"If anyone would be first, he must be last of all and servant of all"** (Mark 9:35 ESV). **"I chose you and appointed you that you should go and bear fruit and that your fruit should abide"** (John 15:16 ESV).

You might be called to some specific purpose beyond all this, but you can start here and say with the psalmist: "I have a purpose. The Lord will fulfill his purpose for me."

**June 6**

## What gives, God?
Jon Enter

In the book of Job, Job expressed his pain in chapter 10: **"I loathe my very life; therefore I will give free rein to my complaint and speak out in the bitterness of my soul"** (verse 1). Do you know what that feels like? Do you know what it's like to have the hurt continue? That was Job. In chapter 1, he lost his flocks, servants, livelihood, and—worst of all—his children. In chapter 2, he lost his health. In chapter 10, Job was worn down and weary. In this verse, against whom was Job uncorking his complaints and bitterness? God. Job knew God was almighty, and yet his suffering stayed.

When have you been there? When have you thrown up your complaints against God and said, "I can't anymore! God, what gives? Where are you?"

You know what's remarkable? God wasn't angry at Job's painful questioning. Job still knew God was real and powerful. God isn't afraid or offended by your questions, doubts, or confusion of what his plan is either. He wants you to come to him continually.

God is shaping you. Sometimes that shaping is painful, but there's a purpose. God's got a plan. Cry out to Jesus with your uncertainties. But then follow up with these words: "Form and shape me, Lord." He is, and he will.

May God give you the endurance needed to be reshaped by his hand and the wisdom to know what his plan is for you when he's done.

**June 7**

## How often should you receive Lord's Supper?

Daron Lindemann

How often should you receive Lord's Supper?

When I was a kid, my church offered it once a month. It was my family tradition to attend every other time. The church I currently serve offers it twice a month, and my family attends every time.

So where exactly is the biblical instruction about how often to receive Lord's Supper? Here it is: **"Whenever you eat this bread and drink this cup"** (1 Corinthians 11:26).

There is no command about how often. It's Christian freedom. But choose wisely. This meal is a gracious, powerful gift of Jesus' body and blood that washes away sins, delivers from death and the devil, and gives victorious life and eternal salvation to all who believe.

Some churches offer Lord's Supper every Sunday. That's good. So why not every day? Well, practical limitations come into play. And good spiritual interests.

It can be helpful for Lord's Supper to be something special and extraordinary and once-in-a-while as compared to every Sunday. However, that concern can be addressed by making it something special and extraordinary every week as well.

Bottom line: Be thoughtful as an individual and a church about the *why* of the *when* for celebrating Lord's Supper. Teach about it. Talk about it. Make it special. And enjoy it "whenever."

**June 8**

## An answer to anger
Nathan Nass

"Everyone is angry!" A friend recently recounted a conversation with a clerk at a store. Out of the blue, that young lady said, "Everyone is angry!" Isn't that the truth? Horns honk, and road rage bubbles over. Video games encourage players to kill as many as possible. Politics is filled with vitriol. It impacts us, doesn't it? Everyone is angry! What can we do?

Here's what God encourages us to do: **"Turn to me and be saved, all you ends of the earth; for I am God, and there is no other"** (Isaiah 45:22). We need more than different political leaders. We need more than less graphic video games. We need more than better drivers on the roads. We need a Savior. We need someone to save us from our sins. We need someone to save us from ourselves.

Did you see what God offers us? *"Turn to me and be saved, all you ends of the earth."* What a simple promise! The Bible's message to us is to repent—to turn!—to God and find salvation in him. Jesus died on a cross for our sins of anger, just like he died on a cross for the sins of the whole world. The answer to anger is Jesus' forgiveness for us. When we see God's grace, how can we live with bitterness?

Everyone is angry, but there's an answer: Jesus! May God lead all of us to turn to him and be saved.

## God's path is best
C.L. Whiteside

As you read this, I want you to ask yourself, "Are things going the way that I want them to go?" If life is going how you want, then check if you're on God's path or on another path. "Another path" means stepping outside of God's will and not being obedient to his Word. The common thought is: "If I'm getting what I want, why would I worry about obedience?" The answer is because it will always catch up with you and give birth to negative consequences.

On the other hand, if life is rough right now for you, don't let it be because you're on the wrong path. Let it be because God is giving you an opportunity to grow! Obedience may not be easy, but **"commit to the Lord whatever you do, and he will establish your plans"** (Proverbs 16:3). God's path is best! Believe that, trust that, and remember what he's done for you.

I have learned (but still need reminders) that committing, focusing, and asking God what he wants for me is life-changing, unrivaled, and actually gives me more of what I desire. God changes what I want when I focus on him. Psalm 37:4 sums it up perfectly: **"Take delight in the Lord, and he will give you the desires of your heart."**

June 10

## The champion
Ann Jahns

My 88-year-old mom is a fervent fan of her local major league baseball team. She faithfully watches every game, even the replays, despite knowing the outcome. Each season, it's my wish that she will see her team become world champions. It hasn't yet happened, so she shelves her hopes until the next year.

Even if my mom's favorite team does become world champs, then what? The pressure to defend their title would begin before the trophy could even gather dust. And with inevitable loss comes disappointment. You can't stay on top forever.

What a contrast to Jesus, our resurrected Easter champion! He defeated an enemy much more powerful than our favorite team's league rivals. When he rose from the dead, he declared his absolute dominance over the triple threat of sin, death, and the devil.

Today believers worldwide exult in Jesus' decisive victory, won once and for all. First Peter 3:18,19 declares: **"Christ also suffered once for sins, the righteous for the unrighteous, to bring you to God. He was put to death in the body but made alive in the Spirit. After being made alive, he went and made proclamation to the imprisoned spirits."**

And Jesus didn't just win the victory. He also made us the victors: **"Thanks be to God! He gives us the victory through our Lord Jesus Christ"** (1 Corinthians 15:57). We don't have to sit in the stands or in front of the TV breathless with anxiety about the outcome of this battle. It has been decided. Jesus is the victor, our eternal champion!

**June 11**

# The name above every name
Dave Scharf

*Child of God.* What an amazing title! As God's children, we await our brother Jesus to come again to escort us to our heavenly mansion. What a blessing to be called a child of God! If you're like me though, it's easy to think about my sinful thoughts and selfish words, and it doesn't feel like a fitting title.

But that's precisely why God sent Jesus! Jeremiah 33:15,16 says, **"I will make a righteous Branch sprout from David's line. . . . Judah will be saved and Jerusalem will live in safety. This is the name by which it** [speaking of God's church—you and me] **will be called: The Lord Our Righteous Savior."** Two thousand years ago, that righteous Branch sprouted out of a manger in Bethlehem, lived a selfless life for us, and gave that life on a tree of wood so that God could continue to rejoice in calling you a child of God.

And because Jesus took our sin and gave us his righteousness, we have been given another glorious name. I wouldn't believe it if God had not said it—"The Lord Our Righteous Savior"! Elsewhere in Scripture, that's the title for the coming Messiah, Jesus. Here, God gives this same name to you and me! So wholly has God forgiven us that he has given us the name of his perfect Son! He sees Jesus' perfection. So be who God has made you to be today! Thank God for giving you the name above every name!

**June 12**

# His name is Jesus Christ
Mike Novotny

About 500 years ago, a 31-year-old man named Jerome was losing his spiritual battle against the devil. While we don't know the details of Jerome's sins, we do know he was in despair, discouraged over his own weakness and seeming inability to stand strong in his faith. That's when an old friend and former roommate wrote him a letter. After giving Jerome some practical advice about how to battle the devil, this friend concluded his letter by writing this: "When the devil throws our sins up to us and declares we deserve death and hell, we ought to [say]: 'I admit that I deserve death and hell. What of it? Does this mean that I shall be sentenced to eternal damnation? By no means. For I know One who suffered and made a satisfaction in my behalf. His name is Jesus Christ, the Son of God. Where he is, there I shall be also.' Yours, Martin Luther."

That is how you and I resist the devil and force his evil forces to retreat. You and I may be sinners, so weak in so many ways, but we know One who suffered for us. His name is Jesus Christ. And where he is, we shall be also.

The apostle Paul teaches us to **"put on the full armor of God, so that you can take your stand against the devil's schemes"** (Ephesians 6:11). Nothing guards your heart and your head quite like the Son of God who suffered for you.

June 13

# Not a day goes by
Jason Nelson

Not a night goes by that I don't lie awake regretting something I've done or something I didn't do. But I greet every morning very grateful to have one more chance in life.

Not a day goes by that I don't battle this old scarred body, but I still fight hard to have another adventure and some victories to celebrate.

Not a day goes by that I don't think about the many students who let me into their lives and influence their faith. And I wonder how they are doing.

Not a day goes by that I ever want to be away from my wife. Not ever.

Not a day goes by that I don't mourn the absence of some dearly departed ones and some dearly not departed ones and entrust their souls to God.

Not a day goes by that I don't think about Jesus and speak his name in a prayer, sing it in a song, or refer to him in a conversation, because I know he's always there in the shadows.

Not a day goes by that I don't think about the future: of my family, our country, our churches. I see the future in the face of every child. And I have hope.

Not a day goes by that I'd rather not **"make the most of every opportunity"** (Colossians 4:5) and have a little more fun in life, because I know there are fewer days that will be going by.

## June 14

# I have too much charge
Linda Buxa

The other day a notice popped up on my computer screen informing me that my work laptop had too much charge. I laughed because I didn't realize that being connected to the power supply for too long was a bad thing. Apparently, it is. So I unplugged it and used up some of the battery charge.

Later, I realized that Proverbs cautions me about having too much charge too: **"Do not withhold good from those to whom it is due, when it is in your power to act"** (3:27).

Obviously, I want to be connected to God, the source of all power, but do I keep all that power to myself? Am I letting God fill me up but not emptying myself to others? Maybe I focus so much on self-care that I forget about caring for others. Like a laptop that performs best if it uses some of its battery, I perform best when I am using my gifts to serve others and bring God glory. You do too. You have been created uniquely and specifically by God to bless the people around you. So don't store up all those good things. Use them up to help, admonish, encourage, support, and love others.

Then plug back in to fill back up. After all, Jesus reminds us: **"I am the vine; you are the branches. If you remain in me and I in you, you will bear much fruit; apart from me you can do nothing"** (John 15:5).

Father's Day | **June 15**

# A child of God
Nathan Nass

We like to think we have lots of choices in life, but there is one thing we most certainly don't get to choose: our fathers. No son or daughter gets to choose his or her father. Our fathers choose us.

For some of us, that's worked out great. For some, Father's Day is something to look forward to—celebrating Dad! For some of us, it's the opposite. Father's Day just means more heartbreak and pain.

Unless you remember your real Father—your heavenly Father. **"See what great love the Father has lavished on us, that we should be called children of God! And that is what we are! The reason the world does not know us is that it did not know him"** (1 John 3:1). See the exclamation points in that verse? This is good news. Great news! In his great love for us, God calls us the children of God.

That's because God chose you. When you were dead in your sins, God your Father chose to give you new life through Baptism. If you've been baptized, you are a child of God! When you and I were powerless to save ourselves, Jesus died on a cross for us. If you believe in Jesus, you are a child of God!

This Father's Day, rejoice that you are a child of God. Chosen. Loved. Cherished. You! "See what great love the Father has lavished on us, that we should be called children of God! And that is what we are!"

**June 16**

## What do you want?
Nate Wordell

What do you want? That's a sharp question. It's not about your body or what you do. It's not about your carefully considered opinion. It gets behind thoughts, right to your heart.

Two thousand years ago, John the Baptist pointed out Jesus. John 1:37,38 says, **"When the two disciples heard him say this, they followed Jesus. Turning around, Jesus saw them following and asked . . ."** Can you guess?

Certainly Jesus cared about their names and their jobs. He was probably curious about their ideas and their habits. But he started with what was behind all that, deeper in than anything else, the thing that motivated them.

**"What do you want?"** (John 1:38).

So, if I may be so bold, what do *you* want? What's at the center of your thought life? What's the goal of your hustling? What's behind your beliefs?

Before you answer, let me remind you what Jesus wants. He had glory and riches in heaven, but his earthly mission was about something else. He had perfect companionship with his Father, but he was after someone else. In his own words: **"The Son of Man came to seek and to save the lost"** (Luke 19:10). Your Savior is after helpless people, and he won't let a little thing like crucifixion prevent him from getting what he wants. Because more than anything else, Jesus wants you.

When Jesus asked two helpless disciples what they wanted, they took off after the One who loved them most of all.

So, what do you want?

**June 17**

# Don't jump off this cliff
## Daron Lindemann

"If all your friends jumped off a cliff, would you jump off a cliff too?" When I was a kid, my mom liked to say that. The conversation maybe went something like this:

Me: "After the football game, I'm going to a party at the Johnson's farm."

Mom: "*Johnson's* farm? Aren't the Johnsons convicted criminals who use filthy language and deal drugs?"

Me, shrugging: "Well yeah, but everybody's going."

Then Mom's zinger: "Well, if all your friends jumped off a cliff, would you jump off a cliff too?"

Hard to argue with her on that one. It's a solid argument. Now that I'm on the adult side of it, I see its wisdom. So here it is: People and circumstances are not always as they appear. Popularity is not always right or good. When that's hard—and it will be—listen to your mom and Jesus (especially Jesus).

Now listen to Jesus' words: **"Enter through the narrow gate. For wide is the gate and broad is the road that leads to destruction, and many enter through it. But small is the gate and narrow the road that leads to life, and only a few find it"** (Matthew 7:13,14).

Jesus chose the narrowest road of all. He did what nobody else could. He died to save you. He walked a road that had never been walked.

Don't follow Jesus based on how everyone else is following Jesus. Follow Jesus based on Jesus.

**June 18**

## My dirty little secret
Liz Schroeder

My dirty little secret: I love watching cleaning videos. There is something so satisfying about seeing a sink full of dishes getting scoured clean or a couch littered with snack crumbs getting vacuumed and lint rolled. What's great is that three hours of work takes 60 seconds to watch!

Did you buy it? That my dirty little secret is watching cleaning videos? If so, I'd like to sell you some oceanfront property in Arizona.*

Would you put your secrets in print? The sins that keep you up at night? The regrettable things you've said that pop into your brain and knock the wind out of you. The vile thoughts that invade your mind—even in church—that would have you rushing out the door if anyone knew.

The enemy of our souls wants us restless, beaten down, and hiding in embarrassment. I wonder if that's how King David was feeling when he wrote this: **"Do not remember the sins of my youth and my rebellious ways; according to your love remember me, for you, Lord, are good"** (Psalm 25:7). God's response? **"I will forgive their wickedness and will remember their sins no more"** (Hebrews 8:12).

You may have a hard time forgetting your mistakes, but God chooses not to remember them. Through Jesus you have a scrubbed-clean heart, a pristine identity, and a blameless new name. So those intrusive thoughts? They're just thoughts. Think on this: **"Therefore, there is now no condemnation for those who are in Christ Jesus"** (Romans 8:1).

* Cowboy hat tip to George Strait. ☺

**June 19**

# The different sounds of thunder
Daron Lindemann

Do you ever wonder why some thunder sounds like a crack, some like a boom, and some like a rumble?

When I was a kid and the thunder sounded, my grandma said it was angels bowling in heaven. *Hmm.* Ready for a better explanation from scientific wonders designed by God?

During a storm, electrical charges build up in the atmosphere. These generate extreme heat in the form of lightning, which megaheats the air around it megafast. This hot air rapidly expands, compressing the other air around it, and BOOM! The sound of thunder.

A "crack" is usually lightning nearby, a "rumble" is a storm further away, and a "boom" indicates lightning that strikes the ground. But there's another thunder that is hotter, more powerful, louder, and more striking.

If thunder were to be afraid of anything at all, it would be this "megathunder." Here it is: **"The Lord thundered from heaven; the voice of the Most High resounded. The God of glory thunders"** (Psalm 18:13; 29:3).

God himself out-thunders thunder. His sovereign power. His ominous holiness. His impactful voice. These don't mean nothing, just like thunder never means nothing. Something. Is. Happening.

Once, when believers were worshiping God, their enemies approached. The Bible says, **"The Lord thundered with loud thunder"** (1 Samuel 7:10), and the enemies panicked.

Boom! God wants your attention. Crack! God strikes down your enemies. Clap! Hey, angels are clapping because this awesome God loves and forgives you!

**June 20**

## In God's presence
Andrea Delwiche

Have you stood mesmerized on a beach as the waves rolled in or taken in the night sky dusted with bright stars? The vastness of these spaces fills your field of vision. Awe refreshes your heart.

We need moments like this with God: Father, Son, and Holy Spirit.

Take a moment to sit in the presence of God, letting his love and acceptance wash over you. Regardless of what haunts your heart, your sins are remembered no more. You are seen and held in God's hands. Jesus, who knows you completely, loves you with everlasting tenderness.

Ask the Holy Spirit to give renewal and refreshment with this landscape of God's grace:

"**You have searched me, Lord, and you know me. You know when I sit and when I rise; you perceive my thoughts from afar. You discern my going out and my lying down; you are familiar with all my ways. Before a word is on my tongue you, Lord, know it completely. You hem me in behind and before, and you lay your hand upon me. Such knowledge is too wonderful for me, too lofty for me to attain. Where can I go from your Spirit? Where can I flee from your presence? If I go up to the heavens, you are there; if I make my bed in the depths, you are there. If I rise on the wings of the dawn, if I settle on the far side of the sea, even there your hand will guide me, your right hand will hold me fast**" (Psalm 139:1-10).

**June 21**

# Ready for "the day of evil"?
Mike Novotny

Have you noticed that your days aren't equally tempting? Some days your mother's personality doesn't bother you that much, but other days you can't put up with it anymore. Some days you don't even think about drinking, but other days you can't think of anything but drinking. Some days you are content with not getting everything done, but other days you huff and snap at anyone who gets in your way. Why are our days so spiritually different? Why does it feel like we are under a spiritual assault out of the blue?

Because the devil isn't dumb. If he sent the same troops to the same spot every day, you'd learn how to defend yourself. Instead, like a clever general, he waits until the opportune time and launches his attack to maximize the damage.

In his desire to save your soul, Paul wrote, **"Put on the full armor of God, so that when the day of evil comes, you may be able to stand your ground"** (Ephesians 6:13). He knew all about "the day of evil," the particular day when the devil would come at you with his every lie, deception, and temptation. That's why Paul told us to be 24/7 protected by the Word of God and the gospel of his Son.

I can't tell you when the day will arrive next. But I can tell you that regular habits of church, Word, and prayer will fix your thoughts on Jesus and prepare you for the day of evil.

**June 22**

# Create-A-God
### C.L. Whiteside

Sometimes I want God to be like Play-Doh or Mr. Potato Head so I can shape him into exactly what I want him to be and do. I guess I wouldn't mind him being like a genie either. Can you relate? We want God to be malleable to our way of doing things sometimes. Thank God this isn't the case!

Nevertheless, knowing we're susceptible to this thought process means we need to move with caution. Second Timothy 4:3 points out, **"For the time will come when people will not put up with sound doctrine. Instead, to suit their own desires, they will gather around them a great number of teachers to say what their itching ears want to hear."** There are many in our world creating new gods or trying to reshape God's characteristics and ways to fit the life they want to live. What our sinful selves *want* and what our spirits *need* are hostile toward each other.

Our God knows best! Isaiah 55:8,9 reminds us how next-level our God is when it says, **"My thoughts are not your thoughts, neither are your ways my ways. . . . As the heavens are higher than the earth, so are my ways higher than your ways and my thoughts than your thoughts."**

We don't need a Create-A-God because the real and best God is perfect love with a perfect résumé. He already created a perfect plan around Jesus. Grow in your relationship with God by praying, meditating on his truths, and studying his ways. See what gets created in you!

**June 23**

## The next cast
Jason Nelson

When I was in the hospital unsure of the outcome of my critical illnesses, I told my children they could sell anything they wanted. Except my boat. Even sick fishermen hope to make one more cast, to feel a tug on the line and exaggerate the size of the catch. To catch fish, one must go fishing.

The words and actions of Jesus embed the ethos of fishing into our Christian identity. We call it other things: evangelism, outreach, service to the community. But they are all intended to *entice* people to become *hooked* (sorry!) on Jesus. He passed the fishing bug on to us when he told his first disciples, **"Once again, the kingdom of heaven is like a net that was let down into the lake and caught all kinds of fish"** (Matthew 13:47). We ought always to be fishing. It's what the kingdom is about.

When I go fishing, I expect to catch fish. I know I need to understand which species I'm targeting and decide upon the right bait presentation. I have a tackle box full of stuff for different tactics. And I have different kinds of fishing rods for targeting different species. But I tend to fish for walleyes with a jig and a minnow, using my favorite pole. And I get mixed results. I could be more creative and tie on something different. I could be more ambitious, hoist the anchor, and reposition my boat. I would probably catch more fish.

Metaphor complete.

**June 24**

## Protect your soul
Mike Novotny

Soldiers don't walk into a fight without the right fit. I'm not sure if soldiers use that slang (fit = outfit), but I can tell you that every soldier cares about their fit. It's why they walk into war zones with assault rifles, tactical vests, and combat helmets. If you want to stand at the end of your next fight, you care about your fit.

Christians care about their fit too. We live in a spiritual war zone with demonic enemies who have clever strategies to kill our faith. That's why Paul writes: **"Stand firm then, with the belt of truth buckled around your waist, with the breastplate of righteousness in place, and with your feet fitted with the readiness that comes from the gospel of peace. In addition to all this, take up the shield of faith, with which you can extinguish all the flaming arrows of the evil one. Take the helmet of salvation and the sword of the Spirit, which is the word of God"** (Ephesians 6:14-17).

We will break this armor down in our upcoming devotions, but notice something about the six items Paul mentions here. Five of them are defensive in nature. Perhaps Paul is suggesting that most spiritual warfare isn't what we do for God (swinging the sword) but instead what we receive from God (the gospel that protects our souls).

There is active combat for you to engage in, but start today's fight by putting on the love, mercy, and grace that God has given you through Jesus. That's how you protect your soul in this spiritual war!

**June 25**

## The belt of truth
Mike Novotny

To prepare you to fight temptation, the apostle Paul encourages you to **"stand firm then, with the belt of truth buckled around your waist"** (Ephesians 6:14). Paul's original Greek could either refer to a belt you could tuck your robe into so you wouldn't trip (like a bridesmaid who holds her dress so she doesn't face-plant during the processional) or to the thick leather "skirt" of a Roman solider that would protect his more sensitive parts.

The truth of the Bible does both of those things, preparing and protecting your soul. The Word prepares you to fight temptation by reminding you of what is good, right, and true. When you are close to losing your cool, the Holy Spirit might call to mind: **"Love is patient"** (1 Corinthians 13:4). When you are tempted to hold on to every dollar God has given you, the Word gets you back to the truth: **"It is more blessed to give than to receive"** (Acts 20:35).

At the same time, God's Word protects you from the "low blows" of the enemy, like when he fixates on your most embarrassing failures and whispers about how unworthy you are. That's when the Word, centered on Jesus, protects you by assuring you that God's grace is greater than your greatest sins.

I am grateful you are reading God's truth today, and I hope it is part of your everyday routine. With the "belt" of the Bible to prepare and protect you, you can stand firm against the evil one!

**June 26**

## The breastplate of righteousness
Mike Novotny

Every Christian soldier who hopes to survive this spiritual war needs these words: **"Stand firm then . . . with the breastplate of righteousness in place"** (Ephesians 6:14). A breastplate was a vest made of either tough leather or iron meant to protect the vital organs. In the same way, righteousness protects the vital heart of the Christian faith.

What does that mean? Righteousness is when you are right with God, when God accepts you instead of rejects you. That is at the very heart of the Christian faith.

No wonder the devil aims most of his arrows at this vital teaching. His strategy is to convince you either that you're righteous without Jesus or that you could never be righteous even with Jesus. He lies, "Someone like you would never deserve to go to hell!" Or he whispers, "You will never be right with God. You don't stand a chance in hell of making it to heaven."

But real righteousness protects you from those satanic lies. No, you aren't worthy or deserving or enough (we're talking about being with *God* forever in *heaven*!). No one is that righteous. But Jesus didn't let that stop him from dying for the world, for relatively decent people and total moral train wrecks. Your past, as dark as it may be, could not stop Jesus from making you right with God.

Remember what you deserved and what Jesus did, and you will have the breastplate of righteousness in its place. You will stand firm in this spiritual fight.

**June 27**

## The shoes of peace
Mike Novotny

Sometimes my daughters and I get into playful pushing matches on the smooth kitchen floor. As the girls have gotten older and stronger, we've noticed that the winner tends to be the one who's wearing shoes. Despite my superior size and strength, wearing socks means I slide backward instead of standing firm when a daughter starts to push. But shoes help me stand my ground.

It's the same for your faith. Paul writes, **"Stand firm then . . . with your feet fitted with the readiness that comes from the gospel of peace"** (Ephesians 6:14,15). Some scholars believe that ancient Roman soldiers had small nails on the bottom of their sandals (like modern cleats) so they could stand firm during hand-to-hand combat. According to Paul, the "gospel of peace" makes us ready to do the very same thing.

The devil would love to push you into the past, sliding you into the memories of your sin, idiotic choices, and the people you hurt. Even worse, Satan wants to slide you back into shame and condemnation, the assumption that God could never love you after what you did.

This is why we put on our shoes for battle. The gospel gives you the peace of knowing that the past is past, that your sins are forgiven, and that God loves you unconditionally. Through Jesus you are redeemed, restored, reconciled, reborn, renewed, and righteous in his sight.

Satan can't slide you back like socks on a kitchen floor when you've got your gospel shoes on. Stand firm in the gospel of peace!

**June 28**

# The shield of faith
Mike Novotny

Perhaps the most intriguing line of the apostle Paul's famous words about the armor of God is this: **"Take up the shield of faith, with which you can extinguish all the flaming arrows of the evil one"** (Ephesians 6:16).

Why would Satan fire flaming arrows at you? Maybe because, as some scholars have suggested, a flaming arrow could cause a soldier to drop his protective wooden shield.

This is why the devil loves the lies that tempt you to put down your faith, to discard that childlike trust in the Bible and its ultimate truth. "Doesn't science prove the Bible to be mistaken?" "Would God really say the things the Bible says about sexuality and marriage?" "A God of love would never support the Bible's teaching on hell." Those "arrows" have left all too many souls Bible-less, Christ-less, and defenseless.

Some historians believe that Roman soldiers soaked their shields in water before a battle so fiery arrows couldn't set them ablaze. In a similar way, faith in Jesus can "extinguish all the flaming arrows" of Satan's half-truths. Jesus himself taught us that the **"word is truth"** (John 17:17), and a Jesus who died for us would never lie to us.

Take up the shield of faith, and you'll stay standing the next time the devil fires an arrow at your soul.

## The helmet of salvation
Mike Novotny

Without a head, you are definitely dead. I'm no doctor, but I do believe that the previous statement is scientifically true. You can survive with nine fingers or eight toes, but you can't live without your one head. No wonder Paul, in preparing you for your next spiritual battle, writes, **"Take the helmet of salvation"** (Ephesians 6:17).

What does a helmet do? It is a stiff, hard, protective layer to guard one of the most vital and sensitive parts of your body. Bikers, baseball players, and rock climbers all strap on helmets because they treasure the only mind that God has given them.

In a similar way, the message of salvation protects the spiritual thoughts of your head. This message about Jesus is solid/unchanging, less like a flimsy cardboard "God loves me/God loves me not" and more like an unbreakable Kevlar guarantee: "God loves me!" When thoughts of guilt, shame, and condemnation ("How could I do that?" "Why did I say that?" "God must be so disgusted with me.") threaten our minds, salvation deflects those deadly blows and protects us with the good news of the cross.

Your mind is too precious to waste on futile regrets of your past sins. So, Christian soldier, take the helmet of salvation, guard your mind in Christ Jesus, and know that you are safe because of the ultimate victory of our Warrior and Savior.

**June 30**

# The sword of the Spirit
Mike Novotny

On my right arm, I have a tattoo of a cross. However, if you are standing in front of me and looking at my ink, that upside-down cross looks a lot like a sword. That's no accident. When I preach, I love to roll up my sleeves and hold the Bible in my right hand, a reminder that we are in a spiritual war zone and that God's Word is one of our greatest weapons.

In his classic text on spiritual warfare, Paul wrote, **"And** [take] **the sword of the Spirit, which is the word of God"** (Ephesians 6:17). The Word, like a double-edged sword, pierces beneath the surface and cuts to the heart of the matter. The author to the Hebrews said, "[The Word] **judges the thoughts and attitudes of the heart"** (4:12). I love how the Word gets to the heart of me, exposing the reason behind my sins (often a faulty, diminished view of God) and pointing me to Jesus where I find love unlike any other I have experienced before.

Every time you grab your Bible, you are preparing for battle. The devil may be the father of lies, but your Bible is the truth, the sword that slays that dragon. If you have strong habits of reading the Word, keep swinging that sword! And if that sword has a layer of dust over its sharpened edge, pick it up today and get back to the fight. Because when you take the Bible into battle, you will stand firm and be strong in the Lord!

## About the Writers

**Pastor Mike Novotny** pours his Jesus-based joy into his ministry as a pastor at The CORE (Appleton, Wisconsin) and as the lead speaker for Time of Grace, a global media ministry that points people to Jesus through television, print, and digital resources. Unafraid to bring grace and truth to the toughest topics of our time, he has written numerous books, including *3 Words That Will Change Your Life*, *When Life Hurts*, and *Taboo: Topics Christians Should Be Talking About but Don't*. Mike lives with his wife, Kim, and their two daughters, Brooklyn and Maya; runs long distances; and plays soccer with other middle-aged men whose best days are long behind them. To find more books by Pastor Mike, go to timeofgrace.store.

**Linda Buxa** is a freelance communications professional as well as a regular blogger and contributing writer for Time of Grace Ministry. Linda is the author of *Dig In! Family Devotions to Feed Your Faith*, *Parenting by Prayer*, *Made for Friendship*, *Visible Faith*, and *How to Fight Anxiety With Joy*. She and her husband, Greg, have lived in Alaska, Washington D.C., and California. After Greg retired from the military, they moved to Wisconsin, where they settled on 11.7 acres. Because their three children insisted on getting older, using their gifts, and pursuing goals, Greg and Linda recently entered the empty-nest stage of life. The sign in her kitchen sums up the past 24 years of marriage: "You call it chaos; we call it family."

**Andrea Delwiche** lives in Wisconsin with her husband, three kids, dog, cat, and a goldfish pond full of fish. She enjoys reading, knitting, and road-tripping with her family. Although a lifelong believer, she began to come into a deeper understanding of what it means to follow Christ far into adulthood (always a beginner on that journey!). Andrea has facilitated a Christian discussion group for women at her church for many years and recently published a book of poetry—*The Book of Burning Questions*.

**Pastor Jon Enter** served as a pastor in West Palm Beach, Florida, for ten years. He is now a campus pastor and instructor at St. Croix Lutheran Academy in St. Paul, Minnesota. Jon also serves as a regular speaker and a contributing writer to Time of Grace. He once led a tour at his college, and the Lord had him meet his future wife, Debbi. They have four daughters: Violet, Lydia, Eden, and Maggie.

**Jan Gompper** spent most of her career teaching theatre at Wisconsin Lutheran College in Milwaukee. She also served six years as a cohost for *Time of Grace* during its start-up years. She has collaborated on two faith-based musicals, numerous Christian songs, and has written and codirected scripts for a Christian video series. She and her husband now reside in the Tampa area, where she continues to practice her acting craft and coach aspiring acting students as opportunities arise. She also assists with Sunday school and other church-related activities.

**Ann Jahns** and her husband live in Wisconsin as empty nesters, having had the joy of raising three boys to adulthood. She is a marketing coordinator for a Christian church body and a freelance proofreader and copy editor. Ann has been privileged to teach Sunday school and lead Bible studies for women of all ages. One of her passions is supporting women in the "sandwich generation" as they experience the unique joys and challenges of raising children while supporting aging parents.

**Pastor Daron Lindemann** loves the journey—exploring God's paths in life with his wife or discovering even more about Jesus and the Bible. He serves as a pastor in Pflugerville, Texas, with a passion for life-changing faith and for smoking brisket.

**Pastor Nathan Nass** serves at Christ the King Lutheran Church in Tulsa, Oklahoma. Prior to moving to Oklahoma, he served at churches in Wisconsin, Minnesota, Texas, and Georgia. He and his wife, Emily, have five children. You can find more sermons and devotions on his blog: upsidedownsavior.home.blog.

**Jason Nelson** had a career as a teacher, counselor, and leader. He has a bachelor's degree in education, did graduate work in theology, and has a master's degree in counseling psychology. After his career ended in disabling back pain, he wrote the book *Miserable Joy: Chronic Pain in My Christian Life*. He has written and spoken extensively on a variety of topics related to the Christian life. Jason has been a contributing writer for Time of Grace since 2010. He has authored many Grace Moments devotions and several books. Jason lives with his wife, Nancy, in Wisconsin.

**Pastor Dave Scharf** served as a pastor in Greenville, Wisconsin, and now serves as a professor of theology at Martin Luther College in Minnesota. He has presented at numerous leadership, outreach, and missionary conferences across the country. He is a contributing writer and speaker for Time of Grace. Dave and his wife have six children.

**Liz Schroeder** is a Resilient Recovery coach, which is a ministry that allows her to go into sober living homes and share the love and hope of Jesus with men and women recently out of rehab or prison. It has been a dream of hers to write Grace Moments, a resource she has used for years in homeschooling her five children. After going on a mission trip to Malawi through an organization called Kingdom Workers, she now serves on its U.S. board of directors. She and her husband, John, are privileged to live in Phoenix and call CrossWalk their church home.

**Pastor Clark Schultz** loves Jesus; his wife, Kristin, and their three boys; the Green Bay Packers; Milwaukee Brewers; Wisconsin Badgers; and—of course—Batman. His ministry stops are all in Wisconsin and include a vicar year in Green Bay, tutoring and recruiting for Christian ministry at a high school in Watertown, teacher/coach at a Christian high school in Lake Mills, and a pastor in Cedar Grove. He currently serves as a pastor in West Bend and is the author of the book *5-Minute Bible Studies: For Teens*. Pastor Clark's favorite quote is, "Find something you love to do and you will never work a day in your life."

**C.L. Whiteside** is a sports coach, educator, and podcaster. He has been blessed to work and be involved with people from all different walks of life, meeting some amazing people who have helped teach, guide, and provide him with unique insights. C.L. is married to Nicole and has a baby daughter. Listen to C.L.'s podcast, *The Non-Microwaved Truth*, at timeofgrace.org or on Spotify, Apple Podcasts, or wherever you get your favorite podcasts.

**Pastor Nate Wordell** is a happy son of the King of the universe. He's absolutely smitten with his wife, Rachel, and he's doing his best to raise two little boys. He's a pastor at Wisconsin Lutheran College and was previously at Mount Olive Lutheran Church in Appleton, Wisconsin, and at Martin Luther College in New Ulm, Minnesota.

## About Time of Grace

The mission of Time of Grace is to point people to what matters most: Jesus. Using a variety of media (television, radio, podcasts, print publications, and digital), Time of Grace teaches tough topics in an approachable and relatable way, accessible in multiple languages, making the Bible clear and understandable for those who need encouragement in their walks of faith and for those who don't yet know Jesus at all.

To discover more, please visit timeofgrace.org or scan this code:

## Help share God's message of grace!

Every gift you give helps Time of Grace reach people around the world with the good news of Jesus. Your generosity and prayer support take the gospel of grace to others through our ministry outreach and help them experience a satisfied life as they see God all around them.

Give today at timeofgrace.org/give, by calling 800.661.3311, or by scanning the code below.

## Thank you!